STRANGERS TO CITIZENS:
THE IRISH IN EUROPE, 1600–1800

STRANGERS TO CITIZENS:

the Irish in Europe, 1600–1800

Mary Ann Lyons and Thomas O'Connor

NATIONAL LIBRARY of IRELAND

First published 2008
The National Library of Ireland
Kildare Street, Dublin 2

Cover design: Martello Media

ISBN 978-0-907328-64-3 (paperback)
ISBN 978-0-907328-65-0 (hardback)

British Library Cataloguing-in-Publication Data.
A catalogue record for this book is available from the British Library.

Typeset by Wordwell Ltd.
Copy-editor: Aisling Flood.

Book design: Nick Maxwell .

Printed in Spain by Castuera, Pamplona.

Contents

Foreword

The National Library of Ireland is the repository of the documentary heritage of Ireland. Inevitably, documents and publications generated within Ireland form the bulk of its collections. However, the corpus of material that has found its way to the library from those who emigrated from Ireland, whether during the seventeenth, eighteenth, nineteenth or twentieth century, is absolutely fascinating and often highly inspirational. The library has used some of this material, along with other material drawn from sources abroad, in its exhibition 'Strangers to citizens: the Irish in Europe, 1600–1800', which opened in December 2007. The exhibition was launched in association with commemorations of the 400th anniversaries of the Flight of the Earls and the foundation of the Irish college in Leuven. The content of the exhibition was devised by Drs Thomas O'Connor and Mary Ann Lyons, who have also written this wonderful book. We thank and congratulate them on their exciting and innovative work, which has revealed much that was previously unknown about those who left our shores during the seventeenth and eighteenth centuries. We hope that you enjoy reading it.

Aongus Ó hAonghusa
Director
National Library of Ireland

Preface

Historians of Irish emigration have usually focused on the large-scale movements from Ireland to the United States, Australia and Great Britain in the nineteenth and twentieth centuries. In this book, however, attention is lavished on an earlier, formative phase in Irish migration history. From 1600 to 1800 continental Europe was the main destination for tens of thousands of Irish migrants. This vast transfer of people, resources and skills, involving individuals of all backgrounds, enriched Europe at a pivotal moment in its long process of political and economic modernisation. It also exposed Irish migrants to new ideas and opportunities, and on their visits back to Ireland these migrants carried home valuable cultural and intellectual baggage. This toing and froing helped to ensure that, during the period between the religious wars of the sixteenth century and the Napoleonic Wars of the early nineteenth century, direct European influences were particularly strong in Ireland. Not surprisingly, this was also the period in which European attitudes towards the Irish achieved forms that remained largely unaltered until our own time.

A bewildering number of reasons pushed men and women to leave Ireland for the Continent. The lure of education, employment, prosperity and religious tolerance was, of course, especially strong. So too were the lust for adventure, the desire for change and the distaste for isolation. By the seventeenth century the Irish had achieved an unprecedented level of visibility throughout Europe: on the battlefields, in the docks of major ports, in the university lecture halls, in royal courts, on the streets and even in the galleys. Naturally, their lived experiences varied enormously. A great number struggled to make the transition, and many went under, succumbing, like migrants the world over, to illness, poverty and hardship. Smaller numbers, however, were successful in making a new life abroad and gained the rights and privileges of foreign citizenship. They made a significant contribution to their host societies in war, politics, trade and diplomacy, in particular, but also in industry and administrative reform. Many of the most successful continued to exercise influence in Ireland. Intriguingly, up to the mid-1740s, the Irish colleges, regiments and merchant houses on the Continent functioned as alternative educational and career networks for those in Ireland who found the official Anglican state uncongenial. In this way, Irish migration to Europe, in all its diversity and complexity, was a crucial factor not only in modernising Europe but also in shaping the changed Ireland that emerged after the end of the Revolutionary Wars in 1815.

Over two centuries, the 'outsider' Irish achieved 'insider' status in countries as diverse as Spain and Sweden and came to exercise influence both in their host countries and at home. Theirs is one of the great human stories of early modern Europe and an emblematic moment in the universal chronicle of peoples on the move.

This publication accompanies the exhibition 'Strangers to citizens: the Irish in Europe, 1600–1800', which presents the story of Irish migrants to Europe in word and image through an innovative electronic platform. The book explores migrants' motives for leaving and the means they used to travel. It traces their progress as they established student communities, mercantile networks and military units across the Continent. It also examines how some made themselves professionally indispensable to European regimes. Finally, the immense importance attached to issues of purity of blood, descent and genealogy as the Irish endeavoured to gain access to a world dominated by deference, privilege and hierarchy is highlighted. This migrant story, part of the historical experience of this island, places Ireland at the heart of a world in movement, sometimes in flight and always in search of a better life.

Mary Ann Lyons
Thomas O'Connor

1. Strangers to citizens: the Irish in Europe, 1600–1800

The Irish, an island people, have always been on the move. Outbound travellers have made their mark on faraway shores. Returning migrants and incoming visitors have contributed to the cultural, economic and genetic wealth of the country. Understanding this toing and froing is an essential part of our knowledge of ourselves. Not only does it help us discover how we became who we are but it also provides hints of what we might become in the future.

Of course, the Irish have not been the only people on the move. Migration is part of the human condition, and the movement of people, resources and ideas lies at the heart of human development. However, because of Ireland's peripheral geographical position and its historical experience, migration looms larger in the Irish consciousness than in that of its neighbours.

The memory of the mass exodus precipitated by the Great Famine in the mid-nineteenth century still casts a long shadow. This human haemorrhage was a calamitous loss for the country but it also proved an economic and cultural boon for receiving countries like Britain, the United States, Canada and Australia. The large Irish presence in these countries has played a vital role in the recent economic revitalisation of Ireland.

In a similar way earlier waves of migration from Ireland, which had Europe as their destination, proved influential for both the European countries that received them and the Irish communities that sent them. The most substantial and sustained of these Europe-bound Irish migrations began during the wars at the end of the sixteenth century, and they continued in pulses of unequal importance until the French Revolution. During this two-hundred-year period Irish men and women crossed and often re-crossed the seas between Ireland and continental Europe. Some were escaping economic hardship; others were fleeing religious and political exclusion. Many were on the move out of simple *wanderlust*. Although a great number of those who migrated never returned, not a few managed to stay in touch with Ireland, where they continued to exercise a significant influence. They did this most effectively through the networks and associations that they maintained among themselves and built up over time within their host societies. Subsequent migrant flows strategically replenished already established Irish groups abroad, permitting them to develop into communities and later to integrate, some very successfully, into the receiving society.

Different Irish communities abroad had different origins. The merchant groups in Nantes, La Coruña and Cádiz grew out of personal and professional associations. They were based on marriage alliances, business interests, commercial exchange and technical transfer. Others, like the Irish regiments in the Spanish, French, Austrian Imperial and Swedish armies, had their origins in the complex political situation in Ireland and in the conflicting power strategies of the English, Spanish and French kings. Military migrants were numerically the most important strand in Irish migration to Europe, arriving there in waves of varying size throughout the sixteenth, seventeenth and early eighteenth centuries.

Irish student communities on the Continent grew out of two sets of related factors. On the one side there were the educational, religious and cultural needs of Irish Catholic families, especially at the higher social level, to whom the doors of advancement had been closed at home by the Protestant regimes of the Tudors, the Stuarts and the Hanoverians. On the other side there was the willingness of foreign regimes, like the Spanish, to support Irish student communities abroad. They did this for a combination of complex religious and political reasons, usually with the intention of supporting Catholicism and opposing the English monarchs. As these student communities gradually developed into colleges, they produced clergy and educated laity who went on to play a significant religious and ideological role back home in Ireland and in other European countries. Thanks to the clerics and professionals who returned to Ireland after their sojourn in the colleges, foreign powers like Spain, France and the Holy See were in a position to exercise

influence there through them. This made the Protestant regimes in Dublin and London wary of movement between Ireland and the Continent, especially when England was at war with its Continental neighbours, France and Spain.

Often closely linked to the Irish student and military communities were much smaller groups and individuals who brought their professional expertise with them to Europe. In the eighteenth century in particular a small number of Irish migrants, thanks to their northern European origins and knowledge of the English-speaking world, came to occupy niche administrative and advisory roles in Spanish, French and Austrian Imperial governments. Their achievement was part of the great exchange of ideas that characterised the Enlightenment. Thanks to their contributions, foreign perceptions of the Irish were greatly enhanced.

| 3

'Push' factors: why leave home?

Irish migrants did not take the decision to leave lightly. Migration was part of a complex set of factors, motivated by social, economic or political dysfunction at home. A series of bad harvests, for instance, was potentially disastrous for agriculturally based communities, leading to food shortages and even to famine. This could provide an overwhelming motivation for whole families, even communities, to move, triggering an increase in vagrancy with serious public order consequences. Large-scale movement of people, caused by famine, was feared by local and regional governments of the time. Their response tended to be heavy-handed. This was the situation in Ireland at the beginning of the seventeenth century and at certain times subsequently, when famine and war created sizeable vagrant groups. The Dublin Protestant regime, anxious to export the political and economic problems caused by war, expropriation and plantation, was usually happy to turn a blind eye to Irish migrants leaving for Continental destinations, even when these were hostile Catholic states. This was especially the case when England was not at war with its Catholic neighbours. Thus, in the seventeenth century, recruitment for foreign armies was approved by the Dublin regime as a way of absorbing demobilised Irish military and vagrants.

Although Irish soldiers were often welcomed abroad by manpower-starved European monarchies, the arrival of large groups of vagrants in foreign ports was a different matter. Also, because migrating Irish soldiers rarely travelled without some dependants, usually spouses and family members, foreign powers had to make provision for them too. In any case the rudimentary structure of the early modern state did not permit an immediate, effective response to this human inflow. Overall, surviving records of the first waves of Irish migrants to the Continent reveal that, although the soldiers were usually welcome, a hostile reception awaited vagrants.

Economic and religious war, of course, was often the immediate trigger for migration from Ireland in this period. The dislocation caused by sixteenth- and seventeenth-century warfare was horrific, especially when accompanied by 'razed earth' campaigns of intimidation and retribution directed at civil populations. The disruption of war in the seventeenth century, in particular, was exacerbated by post-war settlements that involved property confiscation, religious persecution, economic disadvantage and exclusion from education and opportunity. Wartime conquests, consolidated by plantations, not only removed landowners but also impacted their dependants, especially in Gaelic societies where the whole family network was implicated in military activity. Warfare caused large-scale disruption to traditional society and resulted in considerable forced migration. The gradual extension of the London and Dublin regimes' authority to all parts of Ireland up to 1603 and subsequent civil wars and regime changes in 1649 and 1688 ensured, along with the usual economic and demographic triggers, that migration for Europe continued throughout the period. It was the continuity of Irish migration over this time, albeit in waves of unequal importance and with significant lulls, that permitted Irish communities abroad to replenish themselves with new migrants just as the preceding wave integrated and disappeared into the host population. This meant that up to the middle of the eighteenth century the factors and issues pushing the Irish towards Europe remained fresh and topical among the migrant communities on the Continent.

'Pull' factors: why Europe?

However, no matter how violent and urgent the 'push' factor away from home might have been, displaced persons moved about aimlessly unless a specific destination attracted them. It was only when the 'push' factors were accompanied by the 'pull' of a particular alternative location that a real migration flow could develop. The attractiveness of an alternative location was a combination of both the expectation of better conditions and the availability of the means of getting there. The choice of Spain as the destination for the immediate post-1602 migration flows was due to Spanish involvement in the Nine Years' War on the side of the defeated Ulster confederates. After the wars, military, political, religious and economic migrants alike believed that the Spanish monarchy was beholden to them for their participation in the recent campaigns against the Tudors and Stuarts and would provide them with temporary relief at least. There is no strong evidence that these early waves of migrants intended to stay permanently in Spain. Very few, therefore, arrived on the Continent with sufficient means to make their own way. Even migrants at the very top of the social scale, like the Ulster Gaelic lords, moved to Europe on the assumption that they would be supported there and that they would make their way back to Ireland once conditions improved there.

To make the crossing to Europe, Irish migrants hired boats or took ship with merchantmen following existing trade routes. The latter linked the Munster towns, in particular, to ports in England, the Low Countries, France and Spain and gave the merchant elites of the

Irish port towns an important role in controlling and directing migration. This elite was further advantaged by the existence of Irish commercial missions in foreign ports. This explains why, almost immediately after migration became significant in the early seventeenth century, the trading families of the Munster ports, especially, were so dominant in managing migration traffic. Their pre-eminence generated tensions between themselves and migrants from other parts of Ireland, especially those of Gaelic origin. This was particularly the case when competition for royal patronage in the receiving countries stiffened as the number of Irish migrants, of both Gaelic and Norman origin, increased.

Once the migrating boatloads reached Spain, their survival depended on the attitude of local authorities in Spain, the efficacy of Irish lobbying at court, Spanish international policy and, naturally, the level of cohesiveness among the Irish themselves. These fledgling groups, held together by ties of blood, ethnic origin, common interest, ideology and historical experience, remained volatile and did not always develop into communities. Despite the fact that they had often experienced the same set of 'push' and 'pull' factors in coming to Europe, they were frequently divided among themselves, transporting abroad native rivalries and prejudices, local, national, political, confessional and geographical.

Of course, new social, economic and political dynamics entered these *ad hoc* groups as they settled down in their new location and developed into structured communities. The complex interdependency of 'push' and 'pull' factors was gradually replaced by a new set of relations, not only among the Irish themselves but also with the receiving society. When relations with the host society were positive, and even in cases where they were not, integration followed sooner or later. It is difficult to decipher if and how Irish migrant communities, of the merchant, military and collegiate variety, developed and maintained their Irish 'identity'. It is even harder to discover the how and the why of their integration into the host society. Although

we know that particular economic circumstances, political factors and demographic configurations either favoured or hampered migrant community formation and integration, researchers have still to explore and discover how these actually operated.

In some countries the migrant Irish were afforded special status, whereas elsewhere they had to compete with other migrants. The Irish merchant communities in the Spanish and French ports, for instance, competed with trading colleagues from all over Europe. Legal historians in France have revealed the judicial means employed by the French administration to exclude, integrate and control new migrant populations as it saw fit. There was no overarching logic to this: regimes responded to incoming migrants in a largely *ad hoc* and sometimes opportunistic fashion. In this light it is useful to note how issues of natural justice and legal obligation influenced the Spanish monarchy's acceptance of responsibility for Irish noble migrant families in the early seventeenth century. High-born Irish migrants among the Munster Gaelic nobility argued that, because they had been Spanish allies in the war against Elizabeth, the Spanish monarchy now owed them support. The Spanish eventually agreed. Across the Pyrenees in France the successful integration of a number of Irish noble families was aided by the fact that the French authorities decided to grant them equivalent noble status in France, thereby speeding up their integration. Sometimes the only evidence available for Irish claims to noble birth came from the Genealogical Office in Dublin, staffed by officials of the hostile Dublin regime! In other cases claims to noble title depended on nothing more than the good word and testimony of high-placed relations and patrons. Once their noble status had been accepted by the host administration, the Irish enjoyed privileged access to social networks, military preferment and administrative office. Overall, Irish migrants proved adept at presenting the religious and economic grievances they carried from home in a language and form comprehensible to European administrations. Quickly adapting to the political and social environments in which they now operated, the Irish eloquently made their case for special treatment and were frequently successful. They correctly recognised that the Europe to which they travelled, like the country they had left, was a structured political and social system based on privilege and deference. There, the presumption of equality characteristic of modern democratic systems was an alien, indeed sometimes a threatening, notion. The most successful migrants were those who learned how the 'system' worked. They solicited local Catholic patrons, for instance, by playing the card of religious solidarity, often, it must be said, with justification. They also stressed their political and economic grievances against the Dublin and London administrations and particularly in Spain emphasised their alleged common ethnic origins with the ancient Spaniards.

The deployment of inbound Irish migrants in the political strategies of receiving jurisdictions was important. The phenomenon, in all its variety, illustrates how it sometimes suited host administrations to maintain an 'Irish' community, or at least an 'Irish identity', in order to serve specific local political objectives. It is in this light that we can understand the willingness of Philip II and Philip III to endow Irish colleges in Spain and Spanish Flanders as a means of keeping the exiled Irish Gaelic nobility on their side in case they might need their support in future campaigns against England. At the same time the Spanish authorities, anxious to promote trade, were often willing to tolerate Irish merchants in Spain who acted as fronts for Protestant English merchant colleagues. The latter were barred from trading in Spain owing to their religion. In Prague the migrant Irish also proved politically useful. There, Cardinal Harrach used Irish Franciscans as a counterweight to the Imperially supported Jesuits in the 1620s and 1630s. In France Cardinal de Fleury used the services of Irish clerics to help oust ideological enemies like the Jansenists from academic and pastoral positions in the early eighteenth century.

'Irish' identity

The Irish, like other émigré communities on the Continent, identified themselves as ethnically and culturally distinctive only so long as it was convenient or profitable to do so. There were, of course, aspects of identity that they could not disown or, even more importantly, that their hosts would not allow them to discard. In this context the contrast in deportment between older and newer members of migrant communities, the evolution in the policies of the host jurisdiction and changes in the political configuration of the sending jurisdiction were all factors affecting the identity of émigré communities, just as much as fluctuations in trade, international war, weather, and birth, death and marriage rates.

One of the distinctive marks of Irish migration to Europe in the period between the seventeenth and the early nineteenth century was the extent to which the merchant colonies, regiments and student communities were reactions to the stabilising of the Protestant Irish state following the defeat of the Ulster earls and their Spanish allies in the early 1600s. Despite the victory of the Tudors and the Stuarts over the Ulster lords, and notwithstanding the establishment of a fully fledged Protestant state on the island, Irish migrants in Europe retained the aspiration of having an alternative, Catholic regime in Ireland. Like many migrants, the Irish saw their move abroad as a temporary solution to an immediate problem, and they organised themselves on the Continent with a view to returning to Ireland on the crest of a regime change. In this mindset they had set up Irish colleges to educate their children and provide clergy for the native Catholic Church. They had lobbied foreign courts to intervene in Ireland on their behalf. They had also established and entered Irish regiments in the hope that they might one day see action for a Catholic monarch in Ireland. Thanks to these Irish migrant institutions on the Continent, Spain and France could exercise some influence in Ireland when it suited them to harry or provoke the Dublin and London governments. The exiled James II and his successors also availed of the Irish migrant networks on the Continent to feed hopes that a military descent on some part of the British Isles might return the Stuart dynasty to power in Britain and Ireland. Irish Catholics of both Gaelic and Norman origins (along with many Protestant Irish) were firm supporters of Stuart claims to the throne. In the period from the 1690s to the 1740s many of the migrant Irish entertained expectations of effecting regime change at home through the return of the Stuarts. It was not until the defeat of the Stuart force at Culloden in 1745 that this dream was finally dashed.

Conclusion

The demise of the Stuart cause changed the political mindset of the migrant Irish communities and altered their situation *vis-à-vis* European governments. Stuart allies, including the migrant Irish in Europe, became less useful to European regimes as leverage in the negotiation of relations with Britain. More importantly, however, the collapse of the Stuart cause coincided with important social and political changes in Ireland and in Europe, which had serious repercussions on migrant flows to Europe.

By the second half of the eighteenth century, Irish migration to Europe had begun to slow down. Recruitment for the Irish regiments fell; Irish merchant dynasties in European ports integrated; Irish student communities and colleges faced difficulties abroad and later competition from similar institutions at home. These changes were at least in part due to altering conditions in Ireland, which lessened the attraction of Europe as a migrant destination. The anti-Catholic Penal Laws were less rigorously enforced, and from the 1770s some were repealed. By the end of the century Catholics were admitted to the Crown forces and the Catholic hierarchy, terrified of agrarian unrest and republican radicalism, was ready to cooperate with the Dublin and London regimes. This reduced the importance of religious issues as a migration trigger. In addition Irish Catholic merchant elites in the Irish port cities had by then the freedom to build up sufficient capital and influence to finance major infrastructural investment in Catholic institutions at home. This lessened the importance of the older European structures like the colleges. Furthermore, the gradual if uneven penetration of Enlightenment values was taking away some of the bigotry that had made life in Ireland so unpalatable for many Catholics.

Meanwhile on the Continent the old regime was under pressure as the threat of revolt exploded into full-scale revolution in the late 1780s. The egalitarian tenor of the French Revolution spelled the end of the world order based on deference and privilege into which the migrant Irish had been accepted since the 1580s. Their religious, political and economic grievances, historically so crucial to Irish integration into the traditional regimes of France, Spain and the Empire, now proved less convincing. Significantly, the Irish now had alternative migrant destinations. Long before the year of revolution, they had begun to feel the westward pull of the Americas. This grew stronger in the years after the Revolution. Although Irish migration to Europe by no means ceased, the great age of politically and religiously motivated Irish exile on the Continent was over.

Fig. 1 John Speed's map of Ireland (1610). There is a significant disparity between the cartographer's familiarity with the eastern and southern coastlines of the island, on the one hand, and those of Connacht and west Ulster, on the other. This reflected the degrees to which Gaelic territories had been penetrated by the forces and subjects of the Tudor and Stuart monarchs. (J. Speed, *England Wales Scotland and Ireland described and abridged...* (London, 1627 [1632?]).)

Fig. 2 Shipping before Dordrecht, 1651 (oil on panel), by Simon Jacobsz Vlieger (c. 1600–53). In the mid-seventeenth century, as growing numbers of successful Catholic merchants found conditions in Ireland increasingly difficult, they relocated their businesses to thriving ports in the Low Countries, France and Spain. There, many of them very strategically channelled their capital, commercial aspirations and entrepreneurial skills toward exploiting the rapidly expanding range of international commercial opportunities. (Fitzwilliam Museum, University of Cambridge, UK/The Bridgeman Art Library.)

Fig. 3 Cork city and port (1633). Along with Waterford, Cork was to the fore among those Munster ports that maintained particularly vibrant commercial ties with ports in England, the Low Countries, France and Spain throughout the early modern period. From here, several thousand emigrants from a wide hinterland and from all walks of life boarded ship in the hope of a better life abroad. Natives of the city and county were strongly represented among all émigré groups on the Continent, be they beggars, teaching academics, clerical students, merchants or soldiers. (T. Stafford, *Pacata Hibernia* (London, 1633).)

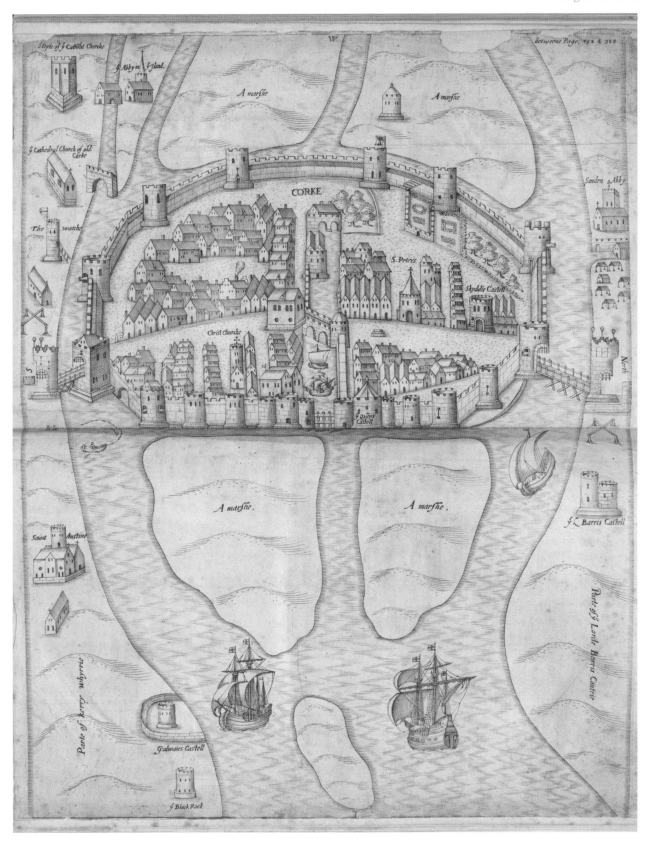

2. Canny mercenaries in *Ancien Régime* Europe

Geopolitically peripheral countries like Ireland, Scotland and Switzerland traditionally produced mercenaries for English and European armies. In 1587, for instance, an Irish force of over 1000 fought in Spanish Flanders, and over the following twenty years up to 20,000 Irish soldiers served in this theatre of war. At the same time the traditional outward flow of Irish mercenaries to England and the Continent was matched by the arrival in Ireland of Spanish and papal troops sent to assist Irish aristocrats pressed by the expanding Tudor state. While the pope was interested in Ireland as a bulwark against the spread of Protestantism, the Spanish, at war with England, were alive to Ireland's strategic importance as the back door to England. The failure of their Kinsale mission in 1601–2 effectively put paid to Spanish military involvement in Ireland. Military migration now resumed its traditional outward direction, but with a new twist. In the course of the Kinsale campaign a sense of obligation was established between Philip III of Spain and Irish aristocrats like the O'Sullivans, O'Driscolls, O'Neills, O'Donnells and MacWilliam Burkes, who had fought with his armies against Elizabeth I. For Philip there was no doubt that 'it is certain the obligation to protect these men and to compensate them for the damage that they received as I intend to do'.

In the pay of their most Catholic majesties

The Irish enthusiastically accepted his offer. By the end of July 1602 the first significant numbers of Munster military refugees began to arrive in La Coruña, often accompanied by their families. Among them were Denis O'Driscoll, lord of Castlehaven, Connor O'Driscoll, son of the lord of Baltimore, Ellen Ní Donoghoe, wife of Dermot McCarthy, who was brother of the ruling McCarty Reagh, and some forty others. In July 1603 the MacWilliam Burke (d. 1604) arrived there, followed, in September 1604, by O'Sullivan Bear. In the interim, others like the baron of Leitrim and Captain Hugh Mosten disembarked and headed for the

Spanish court. The increasing number of Irish arrivals led the Spanish to set up the office of Irish Protector in April 1604. This position was given to the Conde de Puñonrostro (d. 1610), and the Spanish council of state appointed Florence Conry (d. 1629), the Connacht-born Franciscan, as his adviser.

These military migrants and their dependants had a rough passage, some spending several weeks on the high seas. A company of 139 soldiers, for instance, chartered a boat from Kinsale to La Coruña in October 1605 and arrived in Spain starving. When one of the Irish captains was asked why he had come to Spain, he replied that 'as the enemy had taken away all his property and he had always served the King of Spain … for this reason he was happy to be in Spain'. It is difficult to establish exactly how many came to Spain at this time. We know that there were some sixty Irish soldiers in various Spanish companies in September 1602. By June 1605 there were 377, and by February 1606 the number stood at 892. Records reveal that in December 1605 some 769 Irish were receiving financial help from the Spanish Crown. Many, of course, received no aid, and the records rarely acknowledge the spouses, children and hangers-on who accompanied the soldiers.

The Spanish now considered the possibility of establishing Irish units in the Spanish army to absorb the Irish military influx. They were to be put under the command of Irish aristocrats who had recently led Irish confederate forces in the Nine Years' War. Already in mid-1603 Captain Hugh Mosten had been commanded to form a company in La Coruña from among the 400 Irish soldiers stationed in the kingdoms of Galicia and Castile. The following June a second company, of 200, was formed under Richard de Burg. In 1604 there was talk among the Spanish of forming an Irish regiment, or *tercio,* in the Spanish army in Flanders, possibly under the command of Hugh O'Neill's son Henry. When this was first suggested the Spaniards were in two minds. On the one hand, they did not want to jeopardise the new peace treaty with England (1604) by appearing to support the enemies of the recently deceased English queen. On the other hand, there was a pressing need to resolve the practical problem of the influx of Irish soldiers, supplicants and their followers. Florence Conry persuaded Philip III to agree in September 1605 to the appointment of Henry O'Neill as head of an Irish unit in Flanders. It comprised over 1600 men. The formation of the unit enabled the Spanish Crown to channel some Irish migrants away from Iberia towards Spanish Flanders. Between 1605 and 1659, at least fourteen Irish regiments were formed in Flanders, of which seven survived more than four years.

While soldiers were absorbed into the newly formed military units, the Spanish authorities attempted to repatriate, forcibly if necessary, the soldiers' dependants and hangers-on, whom they called the *gente inútil* ('useless people'). This created moral problems for the Spanish authorities, who asserted that, despite the 'danger of persecution', they were 'sending them back to their land for their own good and not because His Majesty wished to abandon them'. The Conde de Caraçena was ordered to treat the matter sensitively and to obtain the approval of the Irish nobility in Galicia before proceeding. The proposal met with predictable opposition from the Irish community. Nevertheless, some of the principal members of the Irish nobility eventually signed a letter stating that 'it seems profitable to us to send back to Ireland all the people who want to go there from among the *gente inútil* such as women, children, old and principally single girls, who have insufficient means to remain [in Spain] notwithstanding the persecution [in Ireland]'. The Irish Jesuit James Archer, while agreeing that the *gente inútil* could be sent back to Ireland 'in good conscience and without danger', submitted a petition to the Conde de Caraçena, begging that children from ten years upwards be excluded from the proposal. Archer suggested that they could be educated in the arts at one of the Irish colleges or trained in some manual skill. The Spanish government relented. In the end some seventy Irish children were adopted by various religious institutions in Galicia even though most of them were not orphans.

In the following decades the Spanish, affected by a manpower shortage at home, actively recruited soldiers in Ireland. This was a practice of which the Dublin government approved. It was anxious to export potentially troublesome young men and had already organised levies for the Swedish army. For hard-pressed Catholic families the option of joining the Spanish army was important as it provided a career option for surplus sons. This became increasingly significant as pressure on Catholic landowners grew. During the 1640s the Spanish recruited over 20,000 Irish mercenaries, who fought against the French and the Portuguese and Catalan rebels. Spanish service was notoriously tough, and, once in Spain, Irish mercenaries frequently left to join the armies of its arch-rival, France. This gave rise to serious doubts about the loyalty and fighting efficiency of the Irish units. In the early 1640s, Francisco de Melo, then governor-general of Spanish Flanders, regretted bringing Irish soldiers to the Iberian peninsula. He declared 'the Irish are so badly disciplined … I am sorry that they enter in Spain'. The virtual collapse of Spanish finances after the 1652 bankruptcy exacerbated this movement. Philip IV admitted his suspicion of the Irish in 1653 when he confessed to his spiritual adviser, Sor Maria de Ágreda (1602–65), that 'in … [Catalonia] the Irish have betrayed us, passing most of them over to the enemy, and we cannot trust those who still remain, because at every step they threaten us with doing the same'.

As a consequence of reduced Spanish military activity in the Low Countries after the Treaty of the Pyrenees in 1659, the Spanish authorities carried out several troop redeployments in the 1660s, reducing the size of the army, especially in Flanders. This coincided with the Restoration of Charles II as king of England, Scotland and Ireland, an event that seemed to promise Irish Catholics relief and attracted many Irish soldiers home. The impact of these events was especially noticeable in Flanders. In 1661 there were 1700 Irish troops in the Spanish army there. Within four years the

number fell to a mere 37. The resumption of war in the Low Countries led to an increase to about 300 later in the decade. A number of Irish served in the Italian peninsula, mostly in Spanish forces. There was an Irish unit of about 500 in Milan *c.* 1655, and another was active there in 1694. With demobilisation in neighbouring France in 1697, Irish soldiers tried their luck in Spain, leading to a surge in military migration southwards. The Irlanda regiment was founded there a year later. With the outbreak of the Wars of the Spanish Succession (1701–14), Irish mercenaries were again in demand in Spain. This led to the creation of the Ultonia and Hibernia regiments in 1709. The accession of the French Bourbons to the Spanish throne facilitated the transfer of Irish troops between the two kingdoms. In the first two decades of the eighteenth century, families such as the O'Briens, O'Nellys, O'Reillys, Mahonys, O'Connors, O'Donnells, Lacys, O'Farrells and O'Doyles arrived in Spain to assume military service, the majority coming south with the armies of Philip V, the first Bourbon king of Spain. By 1720 another six Irish regiments had been set up, and by 1758 their strength stood at about 4000 officers and soldiers. In recognition of their service, the king accorded them the privilege of Spanish citizenship. Irish mercenaries used this concession to fuel promotion ambitions, and not a few were successful, despite the strict social stratification prevalent in Spain. The Irish were promoted not only because of good combat records but also owing to their knowledge of military discipline and their specific technical expertise in artillery, engineering and sanitation. They played a significant role in the modernisation of the Spanish armies under the Bourbons, mixing civil and military responsibilities. Some Irish officers who were born in France saw distinguished service in Spain. The most remarkable of these was Ricardo Wall (1694–1777). He was born in Nantes but was in Spanish service by 1718. Later he became secretary of war to Charles III and prime minister. His entourage included the Meath-born Alexander O'Reilly (d. 1794), who served the Spanish

Bourbons as military commander and regional governor. Later in the century the number of Irish rank and file in the Spanish army declined. In 1722 and 1734–6 Irish regiments were disbanded. Subsequently, few Irish rank and file joined up, and the officer corps was dominated by a small number of privileged Irish military dynasties. These regiments were finally disbanded in 1818.

The Austrian Habsburgs emulated their Spanish cousins in employing Irish mercenaries. The first Irish regiment in Austrian service was in existence by 1630, under the command of Sir James Butler. His brother Walter later recruited his own regiment of dragoons and won notoriety for his part in the spectacular assassination of the Imperial general Albrecht von Wallenstein in 1634. Irish officers enjoyed good promotion prospects in Austrian service, especially in the eighteenth century. Emperor Francis I (d. 1768) famously stated 'the more Irish officers in the Austrian service the better; our troops will always be disciplined; an Irish coward is an uncommon character'. In the mid-eighteenth century Field Marshal Count Francis Maurice Lacy was president of the council of war. In 1766, on St Patrick's Day, the Spanish ambassador at Vienna, Count O'Mahony, received Count Lacy, generals O'Donnell, Maguire, O'Kelly, Browne, Plunkett and MacElligott and a number of other senior military figures claiming Irish extraction. In a petition to Empress Maria Theresa (1717–80), Viscount Nicholas Taaffe (b. 1685) underlined the role that foreign service played in maintaining the fortunes of beleaguered Catholic landowning families in Ireland, who could provide no prospects whatsoever for younger sons. He explained that he had left Ireland:

> Because he was afraid that his descendants pressed by the penal laws would not resist the temptation of becoming protestants. He therefore took refuge to a catholic country where his ancestors were well known for the military service they had rendered at different intervals to the House of Austria. He had

abandoned his relations and his estates and the rank and liberty he had in his own country to prevent his descendants from deserting a religion to which their Imperial majesties so fervently adhered.

To a greater extent than in Spain, the entry of Irish rank and file to the Austrian armies dried up long before the Irish officer corps disappeared. At the end of the period Colonel O'Shee, of Kilkenny, who commanded 3000 men for Austria against the Napoleonic armies at Wagram, represented the swansong of major Irish involvement in the Austrian Imperial armies.

Under the Bourbon banner

As early as the 1630s France was beginning to displace Spain and Austria as the main destination for Irish mercenaries and military refugees. Irish soldiers had begun to crop up in French records in the 1590s, when a few, like Dominic O'Collins of Youghal, joined the armies of the French Catholic League. The inward flow of Irish soldiers quickened in the 1630s, and between 1634 and 1660 some 30,000 Irishmen crossed to serve the French king. They fed Cardinal Richelieu's build-up of forces in preparation for French entry into the Thirty Years' War in 1635. Usually with the approval of the Dublin government, military entrepreneurs like the Walls of Coolnamucky, the Butlers, the Barrys in Cork, the Sinnotts in Wexford, the Tyrells and the Crosbies recruited for France in Ireland.

Further recruitment took place in the late 1630s to make up for natural wastage but it ceased for a while at the outbreak of the English Civil War and the Confederate Wars. Irish colonels were allowed to return to Ireland by Richelieu. Only the Wall regiment remained intact in France. Irish recruitment resumed, however, in late 1644, when Richard Bellings and Lord Iveagh sailed with 1000 men from Galway. The MacCarthys of Muskerry took a regiment to France in 1647–8, as did the Prestons, who diverted troops originally destined for Spain. The Cromwellian campaign and its aftermath brought a surge in Irish soldiers travelling to France. Estimates vary, but it is possible that up to 16,000 soldiers left for Spain and slightly more for France during this period. Inchiquin, Ormond and O'Sullivan Beare were among the commanders who sailed for France, and they were soon joined by others, who had originally landed in Spain. Many of them subsequently fled to France from atrocious conditions and bad pay in Spain. Some of these served in the armies of the aristocratic French leaders of the Fronde rebellion, but most joined the French royal army.

From 1656 to 1659 six Irish regiments remained in France, but they were progressively disbanded after the peace between France and Spain in 1659. In overall terms, the proportion of Irish soldiers in the French army varied from 2 per cent during the Thirty Years' War to 5 per cent in the early 1650s, peaking at perhaps 8 per cent in the mid-1650s, when there may have been nearly 30,000 Irish troops and cavalry in France. This figure had dropped to some 2000 after Louis XIV came to the throne. The disbanding of Dillon's regiment—the last of the 1650s regiments—in 1664 did not mean the end of the Irish presence in the French armies. Irish companies, for instance, existed in British and German regiments in the French forces between 1664 and 1688, ensuring an unbroken Irish presence in the French armies throughout the seventeenth century.

The most significant single Irish military migration to France occurred with the Williamite wars in the late seventeenth century. The mass military migration of troops that would later form the *régiments irlandais*, or Irish regiments, took place in two waves. In 1690, in exchange for a contingent of French soldiers sent to Ireland, around 5000 Irish soldiers sailed from Kinsale to Brest under the command of Justin MacCarthy. This group formed a foreign brigade within the French army and as such enjoyed better pay than their French colleagues. The second wave of Irish military migration to France took place after the defeat of the Jacobite forces, supported by Louis XIV in his European campaign against William of Orange. Under the Treaty of Limerick (1691) the Williamite commander, General Ginkel (1644–1703), allowed for the transport to France of all Irish forces who wished to leave. About 12,000, with an unspecified number of dependants and followers, sailed for France. This military group formed a separate army in France under the command of James II and subsequently of his son, James III. The total strength of both Irish groups was about 18,000. When peace returned to Europe after the Treaty of Ryswick (1697), the French army was reformed. Henceforth, the Irish and Jacobite regiments and companies were reorganised into an Irish force in the service of the king of France. As a result of the reform, the infantry was reduced to eight regiments, leaving a total force of 5600 men on paper. The regiments were named after the colonel-proprietors: Albermarle, Berwick, Burke, Clare (O'Brien), Dillon, Dorrington (subsequently Rothe, then Roscommon and finally Walsh), Galmoy and Lee. The cavalry was reduced to one regiment of two squadrons, commanded by Dominic Sheldon.

Conditions for soldiers varied greatly. Boredom seems to have been a major source of frustration and discontent, as desertion rates soared in winter and during peacetime, when the armies were idle. Military wages were not extravagant, being the equivalent of that of a tradesman or a peasant. However, soldiers enjoyed the advantage of receiving pay on Sundays and holidays. The downside, of course, was the higher risk of mortality, from fever in winter quarters and death in battle or as a result of wounds suffered. Soldiers in French military service enlisted for a minimum of six years according to a law of 1682. This term of service was increased to eight years in 1762, but in reality terms lasted from a few weeks to decades. Hugo Macalester, an Irishman in the colonel's company of the Rothe regiment, enrolled in 1691 and retired in July 1735, having served in the ranks for 34 years. Patrick Conner from Mullingar enrolled in September 1704 and was discharged holding the rank of sergeant thirty years later. Another Irishman, Patrice Garmely, served from 1691 to 1731 and died in service. More common were soldiers who left the army after a short term in service. Laurent Caside, the 31-year-old son of an Irishman, enrolled on 20 July 1732 and was discharged one month later. Brian Crowley enrolled in August 1732 at nineteen years of age but died in service that October.

Discharged soldiers faced a bleak future. In 1697 a large number of Irish soldiers were unemployed. Some sought to enter the service of other European powers; others received charity from wealthier compatriots. Vauban, the celebrated engineer, writing to the secretary of state for war, Barbezieux, summarised the problems associated with demobilisation. He reserved special mention for the Irish troops, advising his reader to afford them special treatment:

> Remember also, *Monseigneur*, the poor Irish, they have served very well during this war. They are valourous troops, poor men, driven from their country in the interest of their religion and out of fidelity to their King, they are worthy of compassion.

These pleas fell on deaf ears, and at least some of the disbanded Irish soldiers turned to crime. The judicial archives of St Germain-en-Laye, where the exiled Stuart court resided and a gathering place for exiled Irish military, attest to a climate of violence. One Doran described the situation there:

> The route between St Germains and Paris was not safe, because of them [Irish brigands]; and they added murder to robbery, when they met with resistance. One Irish Jacobite trooper, named Francis O'Neil, was broken alive upon the wheel, for the double crime of plunder and assassination … the town of Saint Germains became almost uninhabitable, through the sanguinary violence of the Jacobite brigands. No sober citizen dared venture abroad at night, even in the summer-time; and, to what extent, pillage and murder were carried, by the fierce and hungry partisans who had

followed the standard of James, may be seen in the fact, that, on one and the same day, five Irish soldiers were 'broken alive' in St Germains, for the crime of robbery and assassination.

Incidents like the seizure of an English vessel near Saint-Malo by a number of demobilised Irish servicemen in 1699 were further evidence of the existence of an Irish criminal subculture in France. Despite the negative publicity generated by such episodes, Irish troops enjoyed a good reputation in eighteenth-century France and were admired for their courage and stamina. Evidence in the *contrôles de troupe* supports this more positive image of the Irish military migrants: according to the records, they tended to be taller, stronger and better built.

In 1715 the Irish regiments were reorganised into five one-battalion regiments: those of Dillon, Berwick, O'Brien (Clare), Lee and Dorrington. In 1744 Thomas Arthur Lally formed another infantry regiment and King Louis XV directed the regiments to reduce in size. By this time the Irish regiments included those of Dillon, Berwick, Clare, Rothe, Lally and Bulkeley. Fitzjames's cavalry (formerly known as Sheldon's, then Nugent's) was attached to a French cavalry brigade. In 1762 the Lally regiment was disbanded. The Fitzjames cavalry was annihilated in the same year at the battle of Wilhemstahl and was subsequently disbanded. The other regiments were reduced to nine companies, each of less than 75 men. The remaining regiments were reformed in 1774 in the face of strenuous opposition from the Irish officer corps. The Clare regiment merged with that of Berwick, and Bulkeley's regiment was incorporated in Dillon's. By 1777 three Irish regiments of foot remained in the French army: Dillon, Berwick and Walsh.

Irish regiments took part in the main conflicts of eighteenth-century France, and some were also involved in attempts to restore the Stuart monarchy. They fought at Cremona in 1702 and at Ramillies in 1706 at the height of the Wars of the Spanish Succession.

Later they saw service in the War of the Austrian Succession (1740–8), when they fought at the battles of Fontenoy (1745) and Laffeldt (1747). The regiments gained a reputation for bravery during these engagements but suffered enormous losses in the 1740s through death and desertion. The losses were rarely made good by fresh recruitment in Ireland. Following a pattern already noted in Spain, from the mid-seventeenth century the rank-and-file composition of the regiments grew less distinctively Irish. Irish recruitment was counted only in dozens per year, and the abandonment of service by cadets and junior officers occurred on an unprecedented scale. Indeed, the very survival of the Irish regiments was now in question. Clare's regiment was imperilled by the death of Lord Clare's son and successor in 1775. The political clout of Rothe's regiment declined with the death of its colonel-proprietor in 1766. With the disbandment of Bulkeley's and Clare's regiments in 1775, the Irish brigade in the French army was reduced in strength. Were it not for the tenacious opposition and self-interested lobbying of the Irish officer corps, dominated by a tight circle of families, even these regiments might not have survived to the Revolution.

As it turned out, they did, but the swansong of the Irish mercenary movement on the Continent was sung not in Europe but, rather prophetically, in the New World. Two Irish regiments participated with the French in the American War of Independence, on the insurgents' side, led by General Arthur Dillon and Comte Antoine de Walsh-Serrant. In 1782 Dillon's regiment laid siege to the fortress of Brimstown Hill on the island of Saint Christopher and was victorious. Major-General Count de Dillon was made governor of the island, and the regiment remained stationed there until peace was concluded. Irish units played important military roles in other arenas of the conflict, especially in the siege of Savannah in 1779. Charles Edouard Jennings MacMahon fought in America and returned to France, where, despite the first tremor of the Revolution, he maintained order in his Dauphiné infantry unit. On his resignation in 1791 he indicated his satisfaction at handing over:

> a regiment which was perfectly intact, which had never for a second been diverted from its love of duty and the strictest rules of discipline ... from its respect and affection for the King and his officers and from its devotion to them.

Mercenary twilight

With the slow death of the European *Ancien Régime*, culminating in the French Revolution, the writing was on the wall for what remained of the Irish military presence on the Continent. This was the fruit of a long historical evolution. From the end of the sixteenth century the Irish mercenary phenomenon was premised on the special treatment afforded the Irish as religious and political refugees from their English-dominated homeland. Even when the Irish formed their own communities in Europe and integrated into European society, they continued to demand and benefit from special treatment. For example, in Spain they persistently invoked their religion and their alleged shared Milesian origins with the Spanish to exercise social and economic leverage. The slow running-down of the traditional privilege-based *Ancien Régime* in the face of economic change and intellectual questioning challenged the special status of Irish military dynasties in Spain, France and the Austrian Empire. It also made Europe less attractive as a mercenary destination. Parallel changes in the Protestant *ancien régime* in Ireland had already caused rank-and-file recruitment from Ireland to the European armies to dry up. The Penal Laws against Catholics were enforced less rigorously or repealed, and new career opportunities opened, especially later in the century, when Catholics were allowed to join British Crown forces.

The impact of these long-term developments was intensified by the series of revolutions that broke out on the Continent in the late 1780s. In France the revolution radically altered the status of foreigners like the Irish. This was the result of the ideological tension between, on the one side, the Revolution's commitment to universality and, on the other, its attachment to a strict idea of French citizenship. Paranoia gripped the new French order regarding nobles, foreigners and Catholics; a law, passed in August 1793, specified that 'the foreigners, born in the territory of the powers with which the Republic is at war will be detained under arrest'. For Irish military dynasties, whose special treatment had depended on their nobility, Catholicism and Irishness, these revolutionary changes completed the long process of decline in the Irish mercenary movement. Irish soldiers would serve the Republic, the Empire and the restored Bourbon monarchy, but the world into which the first Irish military migrants had stepped in the 1580s was gone forever.

Fig. 1 Irish soldiers and peasants by Albrecht Dürer (1521). In the sixteenth century, Irish mercenaries were a feature of wartime Europe. The English poet Edmund Spenser (c. 1552–99), who lived in Ireland, commented that Irish soldiery were 'armed in a long shirt of mayle down to the calfe of the leg, with a long broad axe in his hand…yet sure they are valiant and hardie…very active and strong of hand, very swift of foot, very diligent and circumspect in their enterprises'. (bpk/Kupferstichkabinett, Staatliche Museen zu Berlin/photo: Jörg P. Anders.)

Fig. 2 (a and b) Irish procession at Stuttgart (1617) by Georg Rudolf Weckherlin. Douce Prints d. 44(1), plates 50 and 51 in *Aigentliche wahrhaffte delineatiō vnnd Abbildung aller fürstlichen Auffzüg vnd Rütterspilen…* (Stuttgart, 1618). This procession, which included representations of national groups, was based on a pageant conceived by Georg Rudolf Weckherlin (1584–1653) for the Lutheran court of the duke of Württemburg. The occasion was the festivities to mark the christening of the duke's second son and the marriage of his brother. There was a special Irish segment, preceded by the Spanish parade. The Irish parade included three mounted German heralds, followed by three Irish figures on foot. One of the 'Irishmen' carried an inscription that read *sic spectanda fides*, which was translated as 'thus faith and belief would be freely exhibited'. They were followed by three Irish figures carrying outlandishly large rosaries, three harpists dressed in yellow, two elaborately dressed footmen and their mounted master. A cleric followed with his servant, and then came an extravagant float representing St Patrick's Purgatory. A female character followed, bearing a cross on which was inscribed *solum crede*, which Weckherlin translated as 'belief alone helps with suffering'. She was followed by two footmen, carrying axes, and two mounted figures, followed by four grooms. The extant images of the Irish groups provide a rare insight into early seventeenth-century European conceptions of Ireland and the Irish. This parade was, in fact, a parody of the Irish as Catholics and indicates that the evolution of the stage Irishman at this time was as much the product of European Protestant sensibilities as of English propaganda. Although Continental Protestants were fascinated by the apparent outlandishness of the Irish, they were also repelled by what they believed were their superstitious beliefs and practices. (The Bodleian Library, University of Oxford.)

51

Fig. 3 (a) **An Irish horseman**, engraving in a contemporaneous German publication by Abraham de Bruyn. The Irish enjoyed an international reputation as horsemen in the early modern period. Sir Anthony St Leger, lord deputy of Ireland (1540–8, 1550–1, 1553–6), commented: 'I think for their feat of war there are no properer horsemen on Christian ground nor more hardy nor yet can better endure hardness'.

Fig. 3 (b) **An Irish noblewoman**, from Christoph Weiditz's *Trachtenbuch*, c. 1530. Although Gaelic law allowed women to hold property independently of their husbands, they did not enjoy the right to inherit or pass on land, which belonged to the kin group. Under Common Law, women had no independent right to property. These and other restrictions limited the movement of women. When women migrated, it was always as part of a family or kin group. (Germanisches Nationalmuseum, inv. no. HS 22474, fol. 136.)

In folchem Habit Gehen die 800 In Stettin angekommen Irrlander oder Irren.

G. Koler Excud

Es ist ein Starckes dauerhafftigs Volck behilfft sich mit geringer speiß hatt es nicht brodt so Essen sie Würtzeln, Wans auch die Notturfft erfordert Können sie des Tages Uber die 20 Teutzscher meilweges lauffen, haben neben Musqueden Ihre Bogen vnd Köcher vnd lange Messer.

23

Fig. 3 (c) 'In such attire did 800 Irishmen (or lunatics) arrive in Stettin', engraving by G. Koler (seventeenth century). Gaelic and non-Gaelic mercenary soldiers from Ireland served in the armies of the Protestant Danish and Swedish monarchies during the Thirty Years' War (1618–48). This image of *Irrlander* from MacKay's regiment is probably a depiction of Scottish Gaels. The term *Irrlander* was commonly used to refer to both Irish and Scottish Gaels. (Private collection/The Bridgeman Art Library.)

Fig. 4 Pope Clement VIII (1536–1605). Elected pope in 1592, Clement VIII was wary of Spanish dominance. He cultivated relations with France, which was then emerging from a long civil war. Clement was reluctant to support Hugh O'Neill's rebellion because of the latter's Spanish links and owing to doubts about O'Neill's religious commitment. Although he granted an indulgence to those who fought with O'Neill, he refused to excommunicate those who opposed him, as O'Neill requested. (Museo di Roma.)

Fig. 5 Hugh O'Neill, earl of Tyrone (c. 1550–1616). He was the second earl of Tyrone and the last inaugurated O'Neill. Early in his career O'Neill showed outward loyalty to Queen Elizabeth I while opposing Tudor expansion in Ulster. After his 1598 victory at the Yellow Ford, O'Neill extended his authority outside his traditional Ulster territories. With his defeat at Kinsale, he found adjustment to the new dispensation difficult. In 1607 he made a strategic retreat to Europe, which he probably believed to be temporary. He died in Rome. (By kind permission of the O'Neill Family)

Fig. 6 Queen Elizabeth I, Armada portrait, c. 1588 (oil on panel) by George Gower (1540–96) (attr. to). Under Elizabeth, the Tudor state made a determined effort to bring Ireland under its control. The conflict in Ulster, which threw a shadow over the last decade of her reign, was a major drain on English state resources. In this portrait, which functioned as part of the complex propaganda imagery of the Tudor regime, Elizabeth is presented as 'Gloriana'. (© Woburn Abbey, Bedfordshire, UK/The Bridgeman Art Library.)

25

Fig. 7 The Departure of O'Neill out of Ireland by Thomas Ryan, RHA. On or around 4 September 1607 an 80-ton French ship, captained by John Bath of Dundalk, chartered by Cuconnacht Maguire and carrying salt and nets, arrived in Portnamurray Bay, near Rathmullan on Lough Swilly. This was the vessel that later carried the Ulster earls and their entourage to the Continent. (From the artist's collection).

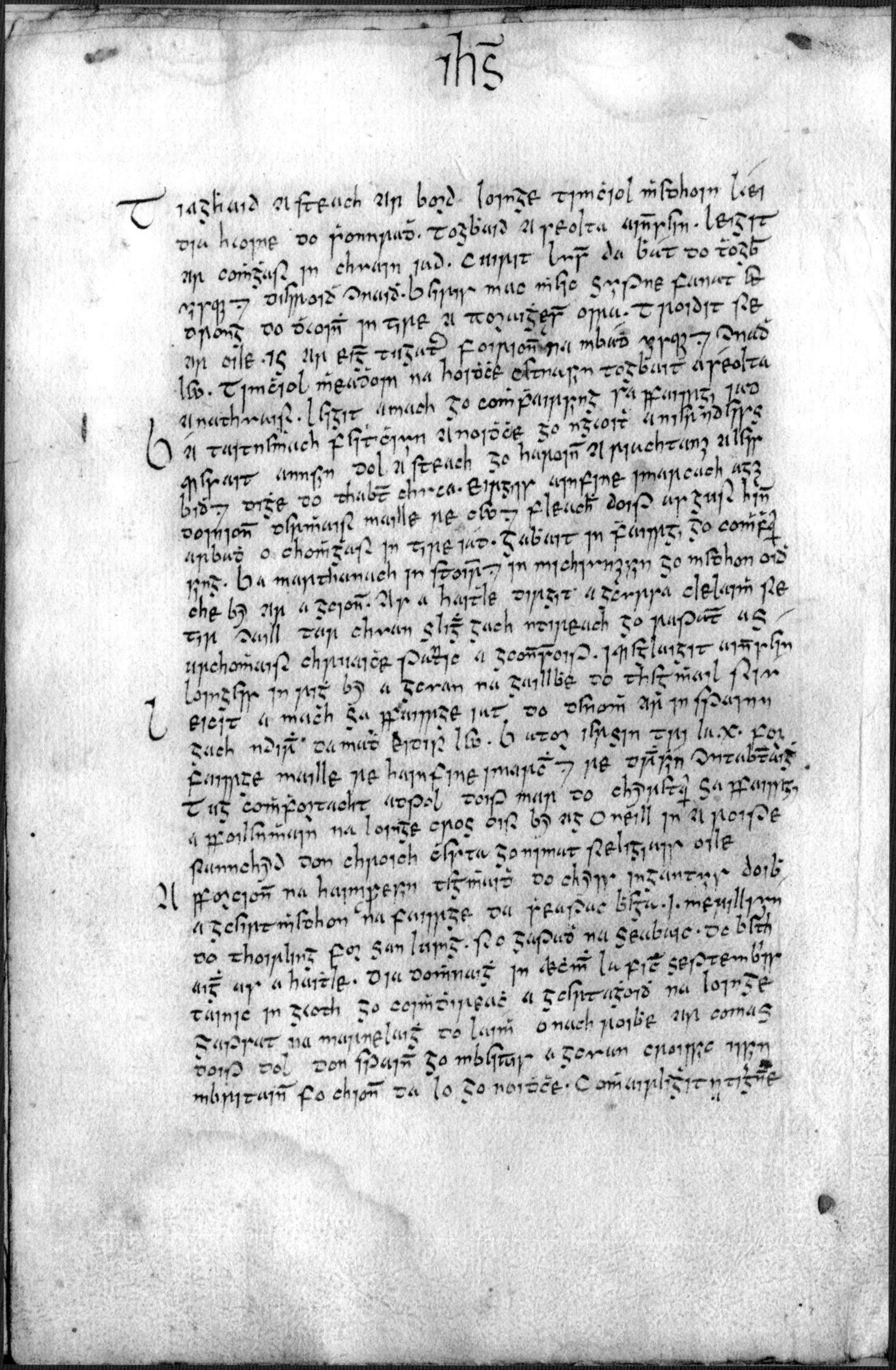

Fig. 8 Extract from Ó Cianáin's account of the Ulster earls' journey to Rome, 1607–8, UCD MS A21. Tadhg Óg Ó Cianáin belonged to a learned family of Gaelic Ulster. He accompanied the Ulster earls on their journey to Rome and wrote an account of their passage. It was probably compiled in 1609 in Rome but was in Leuven by 1658. It returned to Rome sometime after 1793 and came to Ireland in 1872. The manuscript runs to 140 pages and about 38,000 words. (Courtesy of the Mícheál Ó Cléirigh Institute, University College, Dublin, and the Order of Franciscans.)

Fig. 9 Ratification of the Treaty of London (1604). War between Spain and England had been a feature of European politics during the reign of Elizabeth I. This conflict exhausted both countries. With the accession of James VI of Scotland to the English and Irish thrones as James I in 1603, a more conciliatory mood prevailed, resulting in a peace treaty in 1604. After this, there was little prospect of direct Spanish military intervention in Ireland. (The National Archives, UK, ref. E30/1705)

27

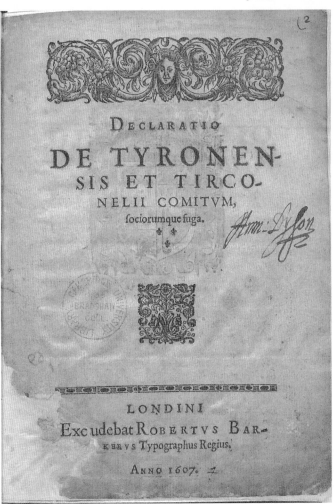

Fig. 10 Title page of *Declaratio de Tyronensis et Tirconelii comitum sociorumque fuga* (London, 1607), an English propaganda piece against the Ulster earls. The so-called Flight of the Earls in 1607 was a diplomatic embarrassment and a potential strategic danger for James I and his government. A strong propaganda campaign was waged against the earls, primarily through the Stuart diplomatic network and also through pamphlets and other printed media. This piece dates from shortly after the earls' departure. (Reproduced by permission of Cambridge University Library (HIB. 7.60.5).)

Fig. 11 King Philip II (1527–98).
Philip II ruled Spain and its empire
during a period of huge expansion.
He was married to Queen Mary I,
and at their request Ireland was
erected into a kingdom by the
pope. Modern-day Daingean in
County Offaly was originally called
Philipstown in his honour. Philip was
anxious to avoid war with England
but eventually sent the Armada in
1588. He founded the Irish college
in Salamanca and played a crucial
role in sixteenth-century Irish politics
and Church affairs. (El Escorial.)

Fig. 12 The archdukes Albert and Isabella, rulers of the Spanish Netherlands. Albert, archduke of Austria (1559–1621), was the fifth son of the emperor Maximilian II. He married the Spanish infanta Isabella Clara Eugenia (1566–1633), the daughter of Philip II, in 1599. In 1595 Albert was appointed governor of Spanish Flanders, and from 1598 he and Isabella ruled jointly. They oversaw the refashioning of Spanish Flanders as a distinctive cultural and political unit. Both generously supported the Irish colleges and the Irish military in their territories. (Musea Brugge. Image courtesy of Lukas-Art in Flanders.)

Fig. 13 Pope Paul V (1552–1621). He was a member of the Borghese family and more closely associated with Spanish interests than his predecessor, Clement VIII, was. Paul V was not enthusiastic about the Ulster earls' coming to Rome in 1608 but bowed to Spanish pressure to receive them. Almost to the end of his pontificate, he was hesitant about appointing Catholic bishops to Irish sees, for fear of government disapproval in London and Dublin. He presided over the completion of St Peter's Basilica and set up the Vatican Archives. (Private collection. Photo © Day and Faber.)

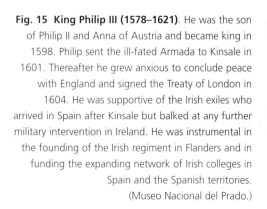

Fig. 14 Letter from O'Neill to Philip III, 9 July 1608, appealing for assistance. Immediately after his arrival on the Continent, Hugh O'Neill made efforts to return to Ireland. Through his agents and correspondence, he attempted to persuade Philip III to assist him militarily or at least to procure his pardon from James I. The Spanish king kept O'Neill at arm's length and, although he was willing to contribute to O'Neill's support in Rome, would not countenance any military intervention in Ireland on his behalf. (Courtesy of Ministerio de Cultura, España.   Archivo General de Simancas. EST-LEG, 988.)

Fig. 15 King Philip III (1578–1621). He was the son of Philip II and Anna of Austria and became king in 1598. Philip sent the ill-fated Armada to Kinsale in 1601. Thereafter he grew anxious to conclude peace with England and signed the Treaty of London in 1604. He was supportive of the Irish exiles who arrived in Spain after Kinsale but balked at any further military intervention in Ireland. He was instrumental in the founding of the Irish regiment in Flanders and in funding the expanding network of Irish colleges in Spain and the Spanish territories. (Museo Nacional del Prado.)

Fig. 16 San Pietro in Montorio, church exterior. This is a view of the façade of the church, which stands on the Janiculum Hill, overlooking the Tiber from the same side as St Peter's. The present building dates from the early sixteenth century. In the seventeenth century this was the nerve centre of Spanish influence in Rome. Irish exiles associated with the Spanish were linked with this house. The Ulster earls were buried here, and Luke Wadding stayed here before the founding of St Isidore's in 1625. (Photo courtesy of Elizabeth FitzPatrick, Department of Archaeology, National University of Ireland, Galway.)

Fig. 17 San Pietro in Montorio, Tempietto by Donato Bramante (*c.* 1502). This masterpiece of High Renaissance art sits to one side of the church. It marks the spot where, according to tradition, St Peter was martyred. Its Doric columns, Doric entablature, dome and sculpted elegance exercised a formative influence on generations of architects. One can only imagine the impression that it made on Irish visitors in the seventeenth century. (Photo courtesy of Elizabeth FitzPatrick, Department of Archaeology, National University of Ireland, Galway.)

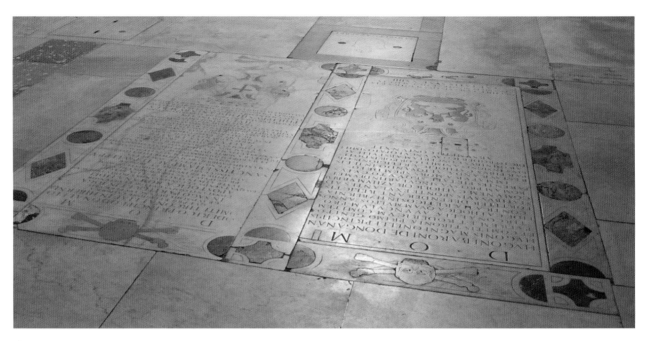

Fig. 18 Tombs of the earls and their families in San Pietro in Montorio. These handsome stones, set in the floor of San Pietro in Montorio, record the deaths of Rory O'Donnell, earl of Tyrconnell, Hugh O'Neill, baron of Dungannon, and other family members. Rory died on 14 September 1608; Hugh on 23 September 1609. The O'Donnell inscription records that when Rory's father, Hugh O'Donnell, Lord of Tyrconnell, died 'in the flower of his youth King Philip III took it on himself to have him buried with honour in Valladolid in Spain on 10 September, in the year of Redemption 1602'. (Photo courtesy of Elizabeth FitzPatrick, Department of Archaeology, National University of Ireland, Galway.)

Fig. 19 San Pietro in Montorio tomb inscriptions. The inscription to O'Donnell begins 'To Prince Rory O'Donnell, Earl of Tyrconnell in Ireland: for the sake of the Catholic faith he overcame many dangers; in peace and in war he was a faithful defender of the apostolic Roman faith'. Hugh, baron of Dungannon, is described as 'eldest son of Prince, the Great Hugh O'Neill, Earl of Tyrone…his untimely death shattered the hopes of many'. (Courtesy of Elizabeth FitzPatrick, Department of Archaeology, National University of Ireland, Galway.)

Top of the Caah

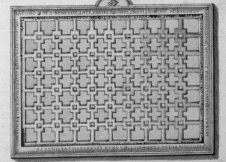

Bottom of the Caah

Fig. 20 Hugh O'Neill gravestone. Hugh O'Neill, second earl of Tyrone, died in Rome in 1616 after years of frustrated exile. He was laid to rest in San Pietro in Montorio alongside other members of his family. The stone that marks his grave is modern and reads 'To the great and good God, the bones of Hugh, Prince O'Neill'. (Photo courtesy of Elizabeth FitzPatrick, Department of Archaeology, National University of Ireland, Galway.)

Fig. 21 The Cathach of the O'Donnells, GO MS 169, fol. 31. The Cathach is a shrine, made for the O'Donnells, princes of Tír Chonaill, in the eleventh century. It housed a sixth-century manuscript believed to have been written by St Colmcille and was traditionally carried into battle as a talisman. The shrine is now in the National Museum of Ireland, and the manuscript is in the Royal Irish Academy. This watercolour illustration dates from 1809. It accompanies a genealogy of the O'Donnells preserved in the National Library of Ireland.

Fig. 22 Donal Cam O'Sullivan Beare (1560–1618). This contemporaneous Spanish School portrait is of O'Sullivan Beare at the age of 53. He joined forces with the Ulster earls when they came into Munster in late 1601 and allowed the Spanish to garrison his castles. After the Kinsale defeat, he held out at Dunboy but then marched north to O'Rourke's territory in Leitrim. He later sailed for Spain, where he was welcomed by Philip III. O'Sullivan was assassinated in 1618. (Courtesy of St Patrick's College, Maynooth.)

Fig. 23 (b) (above) Count Alexander O'Reilly, governor of Cádiz, c. 1780s. King Carlos III sent O'Reilly to lead a Spanish expedition against Algiers in 1775. This proved to be a disaster and provoked an anti-Irish backlash in Spain. A contemporaneous satirist said of him: 'An Irishman sold [us] to the Moors on a sandy beach'. O'Reilly rode out the storm, serving as head of the Spanish military school, commander-in-chief in Andalusia and governor of Cádiz. This portrait captures him during his Cádiz governorship. (Courtesy of Samuel Fannin and Museo Histórico Municipal, Cádiz.)

Fig. 23 (a) (opposite) Don Alexander O'Reilly, governor of Louisiana, by Andres Molinary (c. 1912). Alexander O'Reilly (1722–94) of County Meath joined the Spanish military service. During a term in Austrian service he studied new infantry tactics and on return to Spain gained a reputation as a military tactician and reformer. He juggled military, administrative and political duties during a long career as governor of Havana, military commander of Puerto Rico and governor of Louisiana. This image dates from his service in America. (Louisiana State Museum.)

Frau Königl. Generalissimus Graf Wallenstein Herzog von Fri...
Hr. Hauptm Walter, H. Haupt. Dionisius MacDaniel
die denselben Den 25 Feber 1634 ermord't haben.

Fig. 24 The assassination of Albrecht von Wallenstein (1583–1634) at Eger by a force of Irish and Scottish officers under the command of General Butler, 1634 (gouache on paper), Austrian School (sixteenth century). Von Wallenstein was from Bohemia and served Emperor Ferdinand II in the Thirty Years' War (1618–48). Relations between them soured, and the emperor had Wallenstein assassinated in February 1634. One member of the assassination party was the Irishman Colonel Walter Butler. He died later that year, surrounded by the Irish military chaplain and his fellow countrymen Patrick Taaffe, Thomas Carve and Walter Devereux. Butler made provision in his will for the Irish Franciscan college in Prague. (© Heeresgeschichtliches Museum, Vienna, Austria/The Bridgeman Art Library.)

Fig. 25 Franz Moritz Graf Lacy und Kaiser Joseph II im Lager von Minkendorf. Francis Maurice Lacy (1725–1801) was of a famous Limerick military family that left Ireland after the defeat of James II in 1690. He rose to become an Austrian field marshal and president of the Hofkriegsrat, the Imperial war council. Other famous Lacys included Maurice de Lacy (1740–1820), who was a celebrated general of the Russian army, and Count Francis Anthony de Lacy (1731–92), who had a distinguished career as a soldier and diplomat in Spanish service. In this portrait Lacy is pictured in white alongside Emperor Joseph II. (Heeresgeschichtliches Museum, Vienna, BI 18.879.)

Fig. 26 Franz Moritz Graf Lacy, Austrian School. This portrait of Lacy shows him at the pinnacle of this career. At this time the widowed Empress Maria Theresa teased Lacy that if he did not soon find a wife she would have to marry him herself. Lacy served as Austrian War Minister from 1766 until 1778. He died a bachelor at Vienna. An infantry regiment of the Austrian army remained linked to his name up until the First World War. (Heeresgeschichtliches Museum, Vienna, BI 27.458.)

Fig. 27 Dominic O'Collins (d. 1602), Spanish, seventeenth century. A native of Youghal, O'Collins fought in France and Spain. He entered the Society of Jesus as a lay brother and returned to Ireland. He participated in the siege of Dunboy Castle and after his capture by Crown forces was executed in Youghal in 1602. This contemporaneous portrait depicts him with the instruments of his execution and his martyr's crown. (Russell Library, National University of Ireland, Maynooth, from the collections of St Patrick's College, Maynooth.)

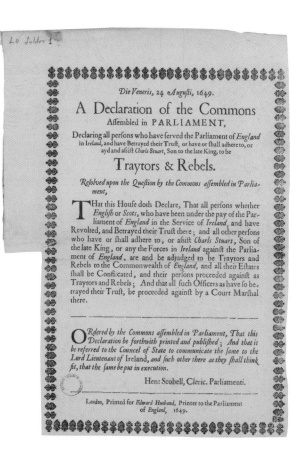

Fig. 28 English parliamentary declaration against traitors, 1649. The Civil War in England and the Confederate Wars in Ireland in the 1640s led to greatly increased military traffic between Ireland, Britain and the Continent. Although Irish soldiers continued to seek service abroad, many returned home from the Continent to fight for faith, country and king. This declaration was issued by the London parliament against those soldiers who fought for King Charles I and his son, Charles Stuart. (National Library of Ireland, Proclamations.)

Fig. 29 Owen Roe O'Neill (c. 1583–1649), Van Brugens (after engraving). A nephew of Hugh O'Neill, Owen Roe joined the Irish regiment in Flanders in 1602 but returned to Ireland after 1641 to lead Ulster Catholic forces in the Confederate Wars. His greatest victory was at Benburb in 1646. He died shortly after Cromwell's arrival in Ireland. (Whereabouts unknown.)

Fig. 30 King Louis XIV of France (1638–1715) by Hyacinthe Rigaud (1659–1743). Louis became king in 1643 at the age of five. Under his leadership France became the most powerful force on the Continent and was involved in three great wars, the Franco-Dutch War, the War of the League of Augsburg and the War of the Spanish Succession. His reign also saw great cultural activity in France. Louis XIV supported James II after the revolution of 1688 and welcomed him and his Irish armies to France in the 1690s, after the Battle of the Boyne. (Photo RMN, © Hervé Lewandowski.)

40

Fig. 31 King James II (1633–1701) by Nicolas de Largillière (c. 1686). James II was the last Catholic king of England and ascended the throne in 1685. He was deposed in 1688 and attempted to regain his throne, through Ireland, in 1690. After the Battle of the Boyne (1690) he retreated to France, where he died in 1701. His followers were called 'Jacobites', and the Jacobite tradition remained strong in Ireland and among the Irish abroad until the middle of the eighteenth century. (© National Maritime Museum, London.)

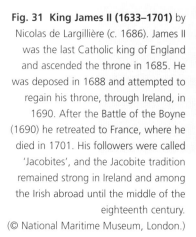

Fig. 33 A solider of the regiment of Berwick (1779) This regiment was founded after the disbandment of a number of Stuart regiments in 1698. The colonel-proprietorship was granted to James Fitzjames, duke of Berwick. It saw distinguished service in all major conflicts involving France, including the American Revolutionary War (1775–83). In 1791 it lost its regimental title and was redesignated as the 88è Régiment de Ligne. (Service historique de la Défense, Bibliothéque, Fonds du Dépôt de la Guerre, MS. A1j 20, no. 91, p. 157.)

Fig. 34 A grenadier of Clare regiment by Seán Ó Brógáin. The regiment of Clare was raised by Daniel O'Brien, third Viscount Clare, in 1689. It was renamed on several occasions as the colonel-proprietors changed. The regiment was engaged at Fontenoy (1745) and later present at the siege of Tournai. In 1775 it was incorporated in the regiment of Berwick. (Courtesy of Eoghan Ó hAnnracháin.)

Fig. 35 (above) The regiment of Lee (camp at Coudun) (1698).
This regiment originated in a number of companies active in Tangiers.
In 1683/4 they were reorganised, and the first colonel was James
Butler, later second duke of Ormonde. In 1685 the colonelship
passed to Justin MacCarthy, who became Viscount Mountcashel. It
was later renamed as the regiment of Lee and finally as the regiment
of Bulkeley. It was amalgamated with the regiment of Dillon in 1775.
(Painted by Percy White from a contemporary illustration)

Fig. 36 (above right) A soldier of the Walsh regiment (1779).
This regiment was originally raised by Charles II in 1662 as the Royal
Irish Regiment of Foot Guards. Until its disbandment in 1791 and
redesignation as the 92è Régiment de Ligne, it saw almost-
continuous service. Like other regiments, it took its name from
successive colonel-proprietors. It was also designated as Dorrington,
Rothe and Roscommon. As the 92è Régiment de Ligne, it served in
the Revolutionary and Napoleonic wars and was finally disbanded in
1815. (Service historique de la Défense, Bibliothéque, Fonds du
Dépôt de la Guerre, MS. A1j 20, no. 95).

Fig. 38 After the Battle at Fontenoy, an engraving by J.D. Reigh (1889), after Horace Vernet. The Battle of Fontenoy was fought in 1745, near Tournai in modern Belgium. It was part of the War of the Austrian Succession (1740–8) and involved French and British forces. Thanks to a dramatic manoeuvre by the six regiments of the Irish Brigade under Lieutenant Charles O'Brien, sixth Viscount Clare, the French withstood an English attack. This won the Irish lasting fame in France. (National Library of Ireland, Prints and Drawings Collection.)

Fig. 39 'Revenge! Remember Limerick— Dash down the Sassenach', an engraving by J.D. Reigh (1886). Irish involvement in the European wars of the seventeenth and eighteenth centuries became an important part of emerging modern national identity in the nineteenth century. This nineteenth-century image portrays the Irish in heroic mode, avenging on foreign fields the wrongs done to them at home, especially the failure by the Dublin parliament to uphold the Treaty of Limerick (1691). (National Library of Ireland, Prints and Drawings Collection.)

Fig. 37 (opposite) The Irish Brigade. The 'Irish Brigade' is the collective title for all the Irish regiments in the service of France after 1691. Brigade members wore red coats in the eighteenth century, with different-coloured facings used to distinguish regiments. In 1757, for instance, Bulkeley's regiment had blue facings, Clare's had yellow, Dillon's had black and Rothe's had dark blue with white braiding. (National Library of Ireland, Prints and Drawings Collection)

Fig. 40 Bataille de Fontenoy, 11 Mai 1745, by Horace Vernet (1789–1863). Vernet was a committed Bonapartist who painted numerous scenes of the military victories of the Empire. Despite this, he enjoyed the patronage of Charles X, who in 1828 appointed him director of the Académie Française in

Rome, where he remained until 1834. Competent in a variety of artistic styles, Vernet is best known for his many large-scale, grandiose battle scenes and military subjects, like this one of Fontenoy. (Photo RMN/© Christian Jean.)

Fig. 41 Richard Hennessy (1729–1800). A native of Ballymacroy, Co. Cork, Hennessy emigrated to France and he entered the French army in 1748. He is recorded in the regimental inspection of Clare's regiment in May 1751. This portrait presents Hennessy as an officer of the National Guard. He was a lieutenant from 1789. He founded the famous brandy house. (Courtesy of the Collection Historique Hennessy.)

Fig. 42 James Hennessy (1765–1842). James was Richard's son. He served as commandant of the National Guard for the *arrondissement* of Cognac. He became a member of the French Chamber of Deputies and a peer of France. James married a member of the Martell family, another name associated with cognac production and the brandy trade. (Courtesy of the Collection Historique Hennessy.)

Fig. 43 Troupes étrangères, legion irlandaise (1810). At the outbreak of the French Revolution there were few Irish troops in the rank and file of the Irish regiments, although officers of Irish descent were not uncommon. A series of reforms effectively destroyed what remained of the Irish identity of these units. From 1796 the Directory considered raising Irish regiments for a planned invasion of Ireland, but it was not until 1803 that an Irish regiment was established for this purpose. (H. Vernet and E. Lami, *Uniformes des armées françaises de 1791 à 1814* (Paris, 1822).)

Fig. 44 Costumes de l'armée française. The Irish served in French armies from at least the sixteenth century, and there were Irish regiments from the early seventeenth century. The Irish regiments were part of a huge French military machine, the colour and diversity of which are suggested by these representations of French military costumes through the ages. (National Library of Ireland, Prints and Drawings Collection.)

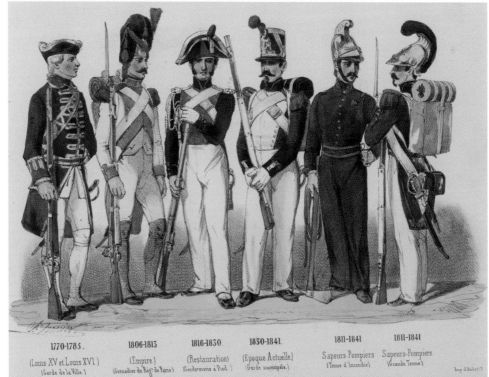

3. Irish student communities abroad

Introduction

The Irish, because of their homeland's peripheral location, were always keen travellers. Political, social and religious circumstances in the sixteenth and seventeenth centuries catalysed these native proclivities, triggering a series of migratory movements from Ireland to the Continent in the period between the religious reformations and the French Revolution. Many of these migrants were soldiers, merchants and scholars. Some were economic refugees, and others were 'political migrants' or 'refugees of conscience' who travelled to Europe in search of the Catholic education that the Tudor religious reforms had made unavailable at home. As religious persecution became a sporadically intensified and constantly threatening reality in Ireland, especially after 1570, there was no possibility of establishing in Ireland the Catholic seminaries and universities prescribed by the Council of Trent (1545–63). Irish students who wished to obtain an education that was congenial to their religious beliefs were obliged to travel abroad. Generally avoiding Scottish and English universities, which were either Presbyterian or Anglican in ideological character, they headed for the great universities of Counter-Reformation Europe, particularly those in Leuven, Douai, Paris and Salamanca.

College origins

From the 1540s Irish student names began to appear in the university registers of Leuven. Initially, they were accommodated in established seminaries or in the fledgling English and Scots recusant colleges in Douai. Later they established their own houses. Between the end of the sixteenth century and the French Revolution, Irish student hostels and colleges were established in Spain, Spanish Flanders, France, Portugal, the Italian peninsula and the Empire. Nearly all of the hostels and colleges began life as small, informally organised institutions. They initially welcomed laity, as well as clergy: they helped to educate members of the lay Catholic elite and acted as centres for Irish merchant and military communities in Europe. They were also politically strategic because, by funding and supporting them, the Spanish Habsburgs and the French Bourbons hoped to exercise influence in Ireland and thereby gain an advantage over their great rival, England. As numbers of Irish students increased, these small, informal Irish student communities developed into proper seminaries with Church recognition and financial patronage from the state, religious foundations or private donors. From a total of about thirty hostels and colleges that survived for more than a short space of time, some twelve were set up by religious orders like the Dominicans and Franciscans, to train their own students. The remainder catered for the training of secular or diocesan clergy and laymen. The latter were often run by religious orders, usually Jesuits.

In Paris six Irish clerics came together under John Lee in around 1578 and found lodgings in the Montaigu and Navarre colleges. The community had a precarious existence until it secured steady patronage in the early seventeenth century. Irish student communities also sprang up in Bordeaux, Toulouse, Rouen, Nantes, Bar-sur-Aube, Wassy, Sedan, Charleville and Poitiers. Most of the earliest foundations, however, were in Spain, Portugal or Spanish Flanders because the Spanish Habsburgs had strategic interests in Ireland and were traditional champions of Catholicism. These territories also had long-established commercial relations with Ireland and thriving universities. The first Irish college to be formally established was in Lisbon in 1590, although the institution took some time to find its feet. Two years later Thomas White of Clonmel secured the patronage of Philip II for a similar institution in Salamanca. An account of 1608 records:

> Father Thomas White … seeing so manie poor scholars of his nation in great miserie at Valladolid, having no means to continue their studie, nor language to begge, having given over his private commoditie, did recollect and reduce them to one place, which he maintained by his industrie and begging, until by his petition to Philip II, in 1592 a college for Irish students was founded.

During the following fifty years Salamanca educated nearly 400 Irish seminarians. The arrival of large numbers of Irish migrants in Spain following the Battle of Kinsale (1601–2) led to a spate of foundations there. In 1605, for instance, Eugene McCarthy founded a private college at Santiago de Compostela to cater for the education of the family and retinue of the Gaelic lord Donal Cam O'Sullivan Beare. Its rather informal discipline aroused the concern of King Philip III (1578–1621), who placed the college under the care of the Jesuits in 1611. Other Irish student communities and colleges existed in Valladolid, Madrid, Alcalá, Valencia, Evora and Seville.

In Spanish-ruled Flanders the Meath-born Christopher Cusack founded the Irish college of St Patrick at Douai in 1594. From it a number of small colleges were set up in Antwerp (1600), Lille (1610) and Tournai (1616). Later communities, some of them female, existed at Nieuport, St Omer, Ypres, Dunkirk and Boulay. The Irish Franciscans were also active in the Low Countries. From the late sixteenth century, government pressure in Dublin had obliged them to set up a network of colleges, friaries and student residences in Europe. Their first dedicated college, St Anthony's in Leuven, was founded by Florence Conry (d. 1629) in 1607, with a professorial corps educated in the University of Salamanca. St Anthony's developed into a centre for the formation of clergy for the Irish mission and for Gaelic-speaking Scotland and consequently developed a speciality in Irish language and hagiography. In 1625 a second Franciscan college was set up in Rome. This was St Isidore's, founded by Luke Wadding (1588–1657) of Waterford. It achieved international recognition as a centre for Franciscan studies, especially in history, hagiography and the theology of Duns Scotus (1266–1308). Pressure of numbers in Leuven and Rome forced the Franciscans to found a college at Prague in 1631. It became an important religious and intellectual institution in the city. The staff of the Prague college, with the approval of the local archbishop, came to dominate the theology faculty of the local seminary. For a brief period in the

1650s the Franciscans also maintained a college in Wielun in Poland. The Irish Franciscan friary set up in Capranica in Italy in 1656 became an important summer residence for Irish friars in Rome. The last Franciscan college founded was at Boulay, near Metz, in 1700 under the patronage of Leopold, duke of Lorraine.

The Irish Dominicans suffered from the same pressures in Ireland as the Franciscans and established colleges at Leuven, Lisbon and Rome. Their Leuven college was founded in 1626. By 1767 it boasted a community of about fifty. The remarkable Dominican Daniel O'Daly (1595–1662), who served as a diplomat for the house of Braganza at the court of Charles II, founded the Dominican college in Lisbon in 1629. It suffered badly in the earthquake of 1755, when it had a community of over 25, all of them Irish. Associated with it was an Irish Dominican convent for female religious, also founded by O'Daly. The Dominican priory of San Clemente in Rome was established in 1677. It enjoyed special prominence in the nineteenth century, when the indefatigable Longford native Fr Joseph Mullooly oversaw the historic excavation of the extraordinary early Christian and pre-Christian remains on the site. The Irish Augustinians set up a college in Rome in 1656, and the Capuchins ones in Charleville (1620), Bar-sur-Aube and Wassy. The Irish Carmelites had a presence in La Rochelle in 1665 and in Aix-la-Chapelle in 1677.

College life

These colleges were small in their early days, rarely housing more than a dozen students at a time. They encountered great difficulty in supporting themselves financially, and many had to close when patronage dried up. The Irish college in Paris had a sporadic existence until it secured, in the 1610s, the patronage of Jean L'Escalopier's (d. 1619) family and was awarded letters patent from Louis XIII in 1623. In the late eighteenth century the two Paris colleges hosted nearly 200 Irish students. The college in Nantes housed nearly 100 students at the end of the eighteenth century. The Irish pastoral college in Leuven, which housed up to 40

students at the time of the French Revolution, benefited from a relatively large number of scholarships, many of which were established between 1692 and 1783.

Students came from a great variety of backgrounds but were drawn mostly from better-off families, especially those with military, merchant or professional backgrounds. Many of them had received some informal secondary tuition, mostly in the classics, especially Latin, in Ireland before departure for Europe. Travel to Europe was by sea, of course, usually from the southern ports, Waterford being especially significant in the early seventeenth century. Students from Meath and Leinster travelled to the colleges in the Low Countries via England, using the ports of Chester and Bristol. Once on the Continent, students tended to be mobile, moving between different colleges and particularly between Spanish Flanders and both Spain and Italy.

Many of the students who travelled to Spain, France and Flanders were mature men in their twenties or thirties. They brought testimonials from senior clergy or from their bishops. A great number of students were ordained before leaving Ireland, and they supported themselves through Mass stipends. They also assisted in parishes around the colleges, acted as chaplains in hospitals and in the army, and gave religious instruction to the children of the local Irish community. Other students were much younger, some barely in their teens. They depended entirely on college scholarships and bursaries for support. All students were required to take oaths of obedience, promising to observe college rules and to return to the Irish mission on completion of their studies. However, many of them, especially those who had left Ireland at a very young age, left the colleges and secured employment on the Continent. They never returned home. It has been estimated that only between one-third and half of those who went to the Continent returned to Ireland. This suggests than some students went abroad not only for political or religious reasons but also because of economic and social pressures. A Continental education was one way for propertied Irish Catholic families to dispose of surplus, second and third sons. This was an important factor when one remembers that, under the Penal code, Catholics inherited not by primogeniture (through the eldest son) but by gavelkind, that is, equal division among all male heirs. This meant that, if surplus sons remained at home, estates risked division and dismemberment. There was real pressure on younger sons to migrate, and their families probably intended that they would not return home, either as priests or in any other capacity.

Students were subjected to a strict discipline, the Paris seminarians in the 1620s rising at 4.30a.m. and following an exhausting timetable until they retired at 9p.m. Students sometimes pursued their studies in the college itself or attended lectures at a neighbouring university or at a local Jesuit house of studies. Those who were not already ordained priests entered the colleges at about sixteen or seventeen years old and spent approximately nine years studying before returning to Ireland. Those already ordained on entry usually spent about five or six years abroad. There were also much younger students, who went to study humanities before taking philosophy and theology courses. Only a very small minority took post-graduate degrees, and a good number took no degrees at all. In the eighteenth century there was a tendency to prolong the period of study. In 1742, for instance, the course of studies in the Franciscan and Dominican colleges was extended by two years. Educational standards compared well with those in other colleges and countries. On completion of their training, the young priests returned to Ireland. Getting trained clergy back to Ireland was not easy. In Spain, on completion of their courses, Irish priests could apply to the Spanish king for the royal contribution, or *viaticum*, granted under certain conditions to assist them in the journey back to Ireland. Between 1619 and 1659 at least 280 Irish priests applied for the *viaticum*, the majority being Dominicans or Franciscans.

The colleges frequently suffered from internal divisions, often caused by poor discipline. In 1669 the situation in Toulouse reached crisis proportions. The local archbishop was informed of:

Various complaints [about] the bad behaviour and scandalous lifestyles of certain Irish priests and students … the constant disobedience they show their house superior, their lack of application in study, at prayer in the evening, in the morning and at mealtimes, their insolence at every hour and in every place, playing cards, indulging in excessive drinking and eating, the liberty they take in receiving strangers in the house as the fancy takes them, leaving the college frequently without permission, visits which may prove suspect over time if they continue, and other licentious ways.

These internal disputes often concerned the selection of superiors. Practice varied between the colleges, but it was not uncommon for students to elect their superiors, usually according to a provincial quota system, which was supposed to ensure representation for all parts of the country. Failures in the system were a constant cause of disharmony and divisions, often along ethnic and provincial lines. The main division was between Munster and Leinster, which both had large Catholic populations of Norman descent, and Ulster and Connaught, where the Gaelic Irish predominated. Because the Irish Jesuits recruited chiefly in Munster and Leinster and were also anxious to gain control of the colleges, there were frequent clashes between them and representatives of the Gaelic Irish. In 1602, for example, the Connaught-born Franciscan Florence Conry, with the support of the Ulster nobleman Red Hugh O'Donnell (1572–1602), petitioned Philip III to remove the Jesuits from the Salamanca college, accusing them of mismanagement of funds, favouring seminarians from their own native provinces and encouraging loyalty to Elizabeth I.

Intellectual achievement

The philosophical and theological education of the students reflected the preferences of the local universities and the college authorities. The Irish Franciscans were especially favourable to the philosophy and theology of Duns Scotus, and their houses in Leuven, Rome and

Prague became important centres of Scotist scholarship. Between 1630 and 1769 about 257 theological theses were defended in St Anthony's, and of these the overwhelming majority (231) dealt with Scotist theology. The Franciscan colleges provided teaching staff for seminaries all over Europe, notably in the Empire, and were instrumental in propagating renewed Scotist theology in the Habsburg sphere. Some of the Irish Franciscans in the Low Countries and Rome, like Florence Conry, Hugh de Burgo and Luke Wadding, contributed to the theological and moral tendencies that later became associated with Jansenism, but in general the Irish of the colleges, both staff and students, were careful to observe the theological discipline favoured by the local establishment.

The Irish Franciscans in particular fostered the study of Irish history, language and hagiography. In the seventeenth century the Franciscan college in Leuven was especially prominent in producing catechetical texts in Irish and in training priests with sufficient linguistic skills to permit them to work in Gaelic-speaking districts. Hugh Ward (d. 1635), Patrick Fleming (1599–1631), John Colgan (1592–1658) and Thomas O'Sheerin (d. 1673) were pioneers in these fields. The extraordinary, if wayward, political activist Peter Walsh (1614–88) was educated in Leuven, and his literary output made him one of the most widely read Irish Catholic writers in England and Ireland in the 1660s and 1670s. In Rome Luke Wadding OFM was a towering intellectual figure of international standing not only for his work on Duns Scotus but also thanks to his authoritative history of the Franciscan order and his activities as consultant to the Holy Office and the Index. Other Rome-based Franciscan theologians included Francis Porter OFM (1631/2–1702) and Francis O'Molloy (*fl.* 1660).

The Irish college in Paris also produced scholars of repute, among them the Meath-born third rector and hagiographer Thomas Messingham (*c.* 1580–*c.* 1638) and the much published David Rothe (*c.* 1568–1651), who became bishop of Ossory. The Gaelic-language poet Thomas Dease (*c.* 1568–1652), later bishop of Meath, was second rector of the Paris college. Michael Moore (*c.*

1639–1726), who bequeathed his library to the Irish college in Paris, was a distinguished, much published late Aristotelian and a critic of Descartes. In the eighteenth century Paris produced a number of theologians, catechists and Gaelic scholars including the Dubliner Cornelius Nary (1660–1730) and Anthony Dunlevy (1694–1746) from Roscommon, the author of *An teagasc Críosduidhe* (1742). The college authorities in the eighteenth century were especially concerned about the linguistic skills of French-educated clergy returning to the Irish mission. They feared that younger students, who mastered French, would lose proficiency in Irish and, when they returned home, would be less effective as priests in Gaelic-speaking districts. Efforts were made to maintain proficiency in Irish: conversation classes were organised, and an English–Irish dictionary was prepared in 1732. The college thus set a precedent for the Gaelic Revival of the late nineteenth and the early twentieth century.

Impact of college clergy in Ireland

In the sixteenth and the early seventeenth century the Continentally educated clergy were unevenly spread in Ireland. However, from an early date they had begun to make a noticeable impact, first evident in the southern port towns from the late 1570s. Sir William Drury, the president of Munster, writing in 1577 to Walsingham, the secretary of state, declared:

> There are a great number of students of this city [Waterford] in Louvain, at the charge of their friends and fathers … by whom the proud and undutiful inhabitants of this town are so cankered in Popery … that they fear neither God nor man, and hath their altars, painted images, and candlesticke, in derision of the Gospel, every day in their synagogues … Masses infinite they have in their several churches every morning, without any fear.

It is difficult to calculate what proportion of the clergy active in Ireland at this time was seminary-educated. In late 1590 Miler McGrath named thirty priests around Tipperary, identifying five of them as 'seminary priests' who had come with two others from Rome. The soldier and author Barnaby Rich (1542–1617) no doubt exaggerated somewhat when he wrote a few years later that the country:

> does swarm with Jesuits, seminaries and massing priests, yea, the friars and these do keep such continual and daily buzzing in the poor people's ears that they are not only led from all duty and obedience of their prince but also drawn from God by superstitious idolatry and so brought headlong by heaps into hell.

From the other side of the religious divide, Archbishop David Kearney of Cashel commented in late 1606:

> we attend to their want in every way we can, and in this we have received great help from those who came this year from the college of Salamanca, who, with their virtue, zeal and learning, labour with marked fruit, encouraging the weak, and exhorting the brave and valorous soldiers of Christ.

Another report of the time mentions that five students of the Spanish colleges were in prison in Kilkenny, three in Waterford and others in Cork, Limerick and elsewhere. In 1607 Lucas Bennet, a Salamanca alumnus, wrote to Richard Conway SJ concerning the renewed persecutions in Ireland. He commented that:

> by means of three or four priests from your College this district is preserved in the purity of the Catholic religion, though they cannot venture out by day and with great risk even by night on account of the spies the heretics have set to watch them.

The following year a report to the Irish Privy Council revealed that:

> the priests land here secretly and afterwards disperse

> … in such sort that every town and country is full of them and most men's minds are infected with their doctrine and seditious persuasions.

Contemporaries noticed the difference between the old, home-formed clergy and the new, seminary types. Eugene Bernard, arriving in Galway in 1606, saw the people attending Protestant service as an error that had 'arisen from the stupid ignorance of some priests who were never out of Ireland'. Educational standards among the friars, many of whom received their formation domestically, were sometimes low, as the Brussels internuncio Bentivoglio reported to Rome in 1613: 'One would hope for more refinement and better doctrine but many of them were ordained in Ireland and consequently lack qualities necessary to the priestly ministry'.

As the seventeenth century wore on, educational provision in the colleges tended to standardise, and their importance as sources of clergy and educated laity grew. By the end of the century all of the bishops and the majority of the priests in Ireland had at least some Continental education. This permitted them to compete well with their Anglican colleagues, who rarely had the same opportunity for foreign travel, overseas education and language acquisition. The returning Continental clergy, however, served a Catholic community that grew steadily more impoverished owing to war and plantations in the seventeenth century and the application of Penal legislation in the eighteenth century. Notwithstanding these difficult circumstances, they acted as an important link between the native Irish Catholic communities and the richer European churches. They also provided their people with solid evidence that they belonged to an international religious community. Although the clergy inevitably acted as conduits for European ideas and fashions to Ireland, all but a very few were intellectually and socially conservative. They were especially wary of social change, opposed agrarian unrest and generally viewed the radicalisation of Irish politics in the late eighteenth century with a jaundiced eye.

College twilight and new dawn

The Irish student communities were volatile from the beginning, subject to the vagaries of international politics and the difficulties of securing and maintaining patronage. However, by the middle of the eighteenth century certain structural problems began to have an impact, which in some cases proved fatal. The difficulties began in Portugal and Spain, where the Jesuits controlled all of the Irish colleges, with the exception of Alcalá. Jesuit dominance meant that the colleges' fate and fortunes were linked with those of the Society. The suppression of the Jesuits in Portugal in 1759 and in Spain in 1767 was something of a disaster for the Irish colleges under Jesuit management. Their properties and archives were amalgamated with Salamanca, which continued to welcome students until the Iberian peninsula fell victim to French invasion under Napoleon in the 1800s. Salamanca was the only Spanish college re-established after the Revolutionary Wars, and, although the diocesan college in Lisbon remained open throughout the wars, it closed in 1834. In Prague the winds of change had also begun to blow. The Franciscan college there, beset by internal feuding, was dissolved by Emperor Joseph II in 1786 as part of his sweeping ecclesiastical reforms. It never reopened.

In France the colleges appeared to be in a more robust condition but were already objects of criticism long before the Revolution. The Irish Protestant writer James St John, who published an account of his travels in France in 1788, was generally positive about the standards maintained in the two Irish colleges in Paris. However, he was hostile towards aspects of Irish student education and formation. Dictation of notes in class, corporal punishment, poor diet and the study of Latin and Irish all met with his disapproval. The practice of spiritual reading during dinner he considered to be 'tyrannical and absurd'. He explained:

> They [the students] are obliged to say prayers at five of the clock in the morning, and to hear mass at half after seven; to say prayers before dinner, and after dinner; before supper and after supper; likewise before class, and after class in the morning, and before class, and after class in the evening. Besides prayers, confessions, and fasts they have another most mortifying institution of a curious nature, called a *retreat* … [during which] they all spend the time in the most gloomy austerity, and in continual religious employment, in prayer and sadness to excess.

St John's analysis clearly reflects his own religious and cultural convictions, but his comments would not have been unfamiliar to advocates of educational reform in France two decades earlier, in the 1760s, when the suppression of the Jesuits had suddenly opened the way for serious change. At the same time the Irish bishops themselves were developing some reservations about the colleges, mostly because of their high level of independence from Irish episcopal authority.

The French colleges negotiated the first years of the Revolution with relative success. However, with the passing of the Civil Constitution of the Clergy in 1790 there was major disruption to Church life, and in 1793 the Revolutionary government seized the colleges and their resources. The subsequent French invasion of the Austrian Netherlands signalled the ruin of St Anthony's and the other colleges in the Low Countries. By 1799 only three Irish colleges were still functioning. This produced a crisis in the supply of priests to Ireland, where emergency steps had to be taken. The Irish bishops negotiated with the governments in Dublin and London for the foundation of a Catholic seminary in Ireland. The Royal Catholic College of St Patrick was founded at Maynooth in 1795 by act of the Protestant Irish parliament. Its establishment meant that henceforth the Irish Church would produce its clergy at home. Consequently, the importance of the Continental colleges, already undermined by the French Revolution, diminished further.

After the French Revolution a number of the Continental colleges reopened. The Spanish-educated Thomas Hussey, first president of Maynooth College and afterwards bishop of Waterford, reflected in 1801 on the role of the Continental colleges in nourishing Irish Catholicism with European influences:

> The insular position of that country [Ireland], the little intercourse between it and the continent might endanger the Catholic faith as taught in that remote corner to dwindle into sectarian forms if not principles too, whereby it must cease to be a portion of the Catholic or Universal religion. Thus different colleges on the continent and the aid if practicable of the regular Orders sent as heretofore as Missionaries to Ireland would be the security against the national faith dwindling into a Sect.

However, other bishops were not so sure. A few years later, in 1803, the archbishop of Dublin, John Thomas Troy, himself Spanish-educated, opined in a more practical, even philistine, tone:

> Were they [the Irish colleges in France] restored to us in their former situation, which they will not be, we could not send students to them from hence without endangering their principles, & offending Government, which we are soliciting for funds to support two hundred additional students at Maynooth, as the like number at present there is totally inadequate to our wants. We daily witness an alarming decrease of clergy. The Almighty in his mercy may in his own good time, restore its ancient government to France, and thereby render our Colleges there useful. It is, therefore, advisable to preserve our rights & titles to them, which, in the worst event, may enable us, perhaps, to dispose of them for a valuable consideration.

This was not a mentality likely to support a full restoration of the Continental colleges, even if this became politically possible. Maynooth was soon providing the bulk of the clergy for the Irish diocesan churches, and the religious orders set up their own houses at home.

In any case, like many Catholic institutions in Europe in the nineteenth century, the surviving Irish Continental colleges tended to become more isolated from the societies that surrounded them, and their role in effecting real cultural exchange weakened. Significantly, Irish migrants now began to target the Americas and the English-speaking colonies as migration destinations, to the neglect of European alternatives. The economic imperative was decisive here but so also were linguistic and political reasons. More and more Irish migrants were English-speaking and were attracted to destinations where English was spoken. Growing nationalist sentiment at home and abroad made Irish movement into Europe both more difficult and less appealing.

By the middle of the twentieth century only three Irish colleges in Europe were still functioning as seminaries for seculars: Paris, Salamanca and Rome. The Spanish college closed in 1951. Its library, archives and artefacts were repatriated to Maynooth. The Irish college in Rome functions as a seminary to the present day, providing a widening range of cultural and educational services to Irish and Italian academics and students. With the outbreak of war in 1939 the Irish college in Paris closed. After the war, it acted as a hospital for US soldiers and later as a home to Polish war refugees. A victim of neglect and cultural contraction, the college languished in a state of near abandon until reinvented in 2002 as the Irish cultural mission to France and Catholic chaplaincy to the Paris Irish. A similar plan is currently being applied to St Anthony's in Leuven, and the old college in Alcalá is earmarked for an educational exchange programme with the National University of Ireland, Maynooth. The historically sensitive adaptation of the Continental colleges to the twenty-first-century educational and cultural needs of Ireland and its European neighbours will demand the same imagination and resourcefulness that animated the original college founders.

Fig. 1 Map of Irish student communities. From the middle of the sixteenth century Irish student communities were established in various European locations. Although many closed in the eighteenth century, particularly during the Revolutionary Wars in the 1790s, a small number survived. The Irish pastoral college in Rome, for instance, flourishes today as a seminary, a house of university studies and a research centre. (Courtesy of Martello Media. Dates given refer to earliest evidence of student community's existence. Boundaries are those of 1648. (Source: T.W. Moody *et al.* (eds), *A New History of Ireland III: Early Modern Ireland 1534–1691* (Oxford, 1976), p. 616, with revisions. By permission of Oxford University Press.)

The communities

War, religious persecution and economic dislocation caused an outflow of Irish students from the 1540s. By the 1570s they were setting up their own hostels on the Continent. Later on, these were linked to local universities. Although some colleges could rely on local patrons, others led a hand-to-mouth existence. They trained priests, housed medical and law students, supported military migrants and acted as networking centres. Through them, European ideas and fashions flowed back to Ireland.

ALCALÁ
Seculars 1579

ANTWERP
Secular 1600

BAR-SUR-AUBE
Capuchins 1685

BORDEAUX
Seculars 1603
Cistercians 1615

BOULAY
Franciscan OFM 1697

CAPRANICA
Franciscans OFM 1656

CHARLEVILLE
Capuchins 1615

COLOGNE
Capuchins 1611

DOUAI
Seculars 1594
Franciscans OFM 1607
Cistercians 1612

DUNKIRK
Poor Clare nuns 1626

ÉVORA
Seculars 1593

LEUVEN
Franciscans OFM 1607
Seculars 1624
Dominicans 1624

LILLE
Seculars 1610

LISBON
Seculars 1590
Dominicans 1615
Dominican nuns 1639

MADRID
Seculars 1629

NANTES
Seculars 1680

NIEUPORT
Capuchins 1627

PARIS
Seculars 1578
Franciscans OFM 1617

POITIERS
Jesuits 1674

PRAGUE
Franciscans OFM 1629

ROME
Franciscans OFM 1625
Seculars 1627
Augustinians 1656
Dominicans 1677

ROUEN
Seculars 1610

SALAMANCA
Seculars 1592

SANTIAGO DE COMPOSTELA
Seculars 1605

SEDAN
Capuchins 1639

SEVILLE
Seculars 1612

TOULOUSE
Seculars 1603

TOURNAI
Seculars 1600

VALENCIA
Seculars 1672

VALLADOLID
Seculars 1592

WASSY
Capuchins 1685

WIELUN
Franciscans OFM 1645

YPRES
Benedictine nuns 1682

IRISH STUDENT
COMMUNITIES

NORWAY

SWEDEN

DUNKIRK
Poor Clare Nuns 1626

NIEUPORT
Capuchins 1627

ANTWERP
Seculars 1600

YPRES
Benedictine Nuns 1682

LEUVEN
Franciscans OFM 1607
Seculars 1624
Dominicans 1624

ST ANDREWS

LILLE
Seculars 1610

TOURNAI
Seculars 1600

GLASGOW

EDINBURGH

DOUAI
Seculars 1594
Franciscans OFM 1607
Cistercians 1612

IRELAND

DUBLIN

ENGLAND

WIELUN
Franciscans OFM 1645

POLAND

CAMBRIDGE

OXFORD

COLOGNE
Capuchins 1611

HOLY ROMAN EMPIRE

ROUEN
Seculars 1610

CHARLEVILLE
Capuchins 1615

SEDAN
Capuchins 1639

PRAGUE
Franciscans OFM 1629

PARIS
Seculars 1578
Franciscans OFM 1617

BOULAY
Franciscans OFM 1697

NANTES
Seculars 1680

BAR-SUR-AUBE
Capuchins 1685

WASSY
Capuchins 1685

FRANCE

SWITZERLAND

POITIERS
Jesuits 1674

NORTHERN
ITALIAN STATES

BORDEAUX
Seculars 1603
Cistercians 1615

SANTIAGO
Seculars 1605

TOULOUSE
Seculars 1603

PAPAL
STATES

VALLADOLID
Seculars 1592

CAPRANICA
Franciscans OFM 1656

PORTUGAL

SALAMANCA
Seculars 1592

ALCALA
Seculars 1579

LISBON
Seculars 1590
Dominicans 1615
Dominican Nuns 1639

SPAIN

MADRID
Seculars 1629

ROME
Franciscans OFM 1625
Seculars 1627
Augustinians 1656
Dominicans 1677

EVORA
Seculars 1593

VALENCIA
Seculars 1672

SEVILLE
Seculars 1612

Fig. 2 The city of Paris in the sixteenth century. Sixteenth-century Paris was a Mecca for Irish students, diplomats and adventurers. Its university, traditionally referred to as the Sorbonne, enjoyed a world-class reputation. It was situated on the left bank of the River Seine, represented on the right side of this map. From the late 1570s a small group of Irish students under John Lee lodged in various colleges attached to the university. (Bibliothèque historique de la Ville de Paris; photo: Gérard Leyris.)

Fig. 3 The college of Navarre was founded in 1305. It was the largest theological college in Paris and disposed of a number of student grants. The first Irish student community in Paris was temporarily lodged there in the sixteenth century. This image by François Alexandre Pernod dates from 1440. (Bibliothèque nationale de France.)

Le Collége de Navarre. (An 1440.)

Nousveaux d'après Pernot

Lith. de Fourquemin

Fig. 4 (a) The Sorbonne was founded in the thirteenth century to support poor students of theology. Because the Theology Faculty of the University of Paris held its meetings in the college, it too, in time, became known as the Sorbonne. A great number of Irish students were awarded degrees by the Sorbonne, and a number of Irishmen, including Luke Joseph Hooke of Dublin (1714–96), were professors there. (Bibliothèque nationale de France.)

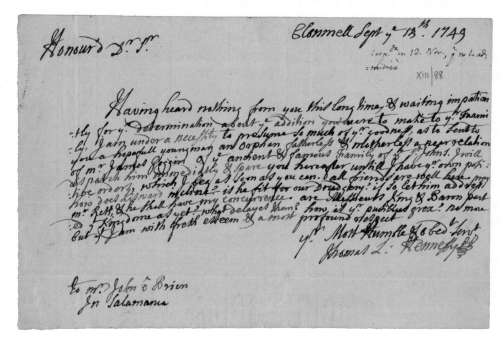

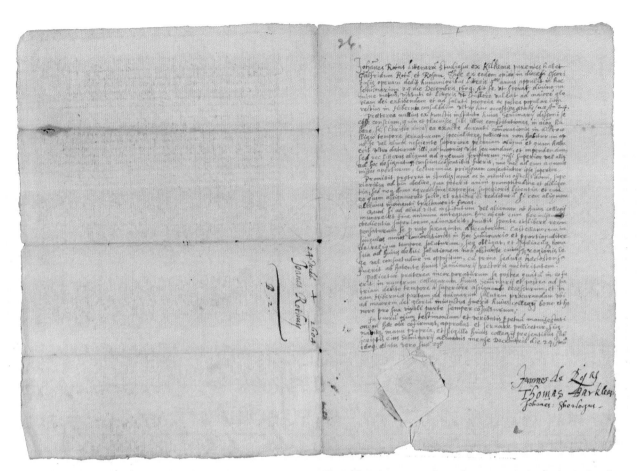

Fig 4 (c) Salamanca college document. Oath of John Rothe of Kilkenny, 24 December 1604. Students in the Irish college in Salamanca took three oaths. One regarded obedience to the college superiors and the house rules. The student also undertook to recoup the college for his maintenance at a rate of 60 Castillian ducats a year if he failed to take holy orders and return to Ireland as a priest. The second oath, taken at the same time, concerned obedience to the college rules. The third oath included a promise to return to Ireland to work on the mission. These oaths, which are more detailed for the earlier years of the college's history, include unique information on the student, his family and his background in Ireland. (Russell Library, National University of Ireland, Maynooth, from the collections of St Patrick's College, Maynooth. Salamanca Archives, I/1/26.)

Fig. 4 (b) Salamanca college document. Letter from Thomas Hennessy, Clonmel, to John O'Brien, rector of the Irish college, Salamanca, dated 13 September 1749. Hennessy writes that he is dispatching 'a hopefull young man an orphan fatherless and motherless a near relation of Mr James Goggin' to Salamanca. (Russell Library, National University of Ireland, Maynooth, from the collections of St Patrick's College, Maynooth. Salamanca Archives, XIII/88.)

Fig. 5 Illuminated address by Paris University to King Charles IX. This illuminated address (1573) is from a collection relating to Scots students at the University of Paris. The bottom right-hand corner contains an image of a group of international students, among which the Irish are listed, alongside their Scots, English, Greek, Hungarian, Polish, Norwegian and other colleagues. This is the first-known image of an Irish student in Paris. (Reproduced with permission of the Keeper of the Scottish Catholic Archives.)

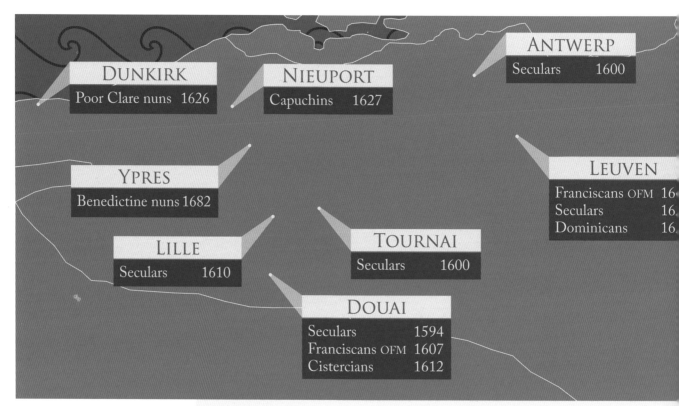

Fig. 6 (a) Detailed map of Irish colleges in Flanders.
Christopher Cusack, a priest of the diocese of Meath, founded
four colleges in Spanish Flanders from 1594. The Irish Franciscans
and Dominicans also founded colleges in Leuven, as did the
archbishop of Dublin, Eugene MacMahon. Other foundations,
male and female, followed. Flanders had the densest network of
Irish foundations in Europe. (Courtesy of Martello Media.)

**Fig. 6 (b) Irish college, Alcalá, account book, eighteenth
century.** Christmas Day and St Patrick's Day were the two main
feast-days of the college year and were celebrated with special
festive fare and double portions. This book contains details of
college expenditure for St Patrick's Day 1723. The community
celebrated with a meal of salmon and rice. Also purchased for the
feast were 'five pounds of sugar, one of almonds, spices, chestnuts
and two pounds of chocolate'. An earlier note records that the
college had purchased a new chocolate machine in 1720. It was
usual on St Patrick's Day for a specially invited preacher to deliver
the homily in the college chapel. In some years the
Carnestolendas, the three carnival days before the season of Lent,
were celebrated. In 1723 eight chickens and one goat kid were
bought, and there were salads and eggs for the pre-Lenten feast.
(Russell Library, National University Ireland, Maynooth, Salamanca
Archives, S34/6.)

Fig. 7 Florence Conry
[Flaithri Ó Maoil Chonaire] (d. 1629). Conry, a Franciscan and Catholic archbishop of Tuam, was founder of St Anthony's College, Leuven. This image of Conry is from a fresco in St Isidore's College, Rome, executed by Emanuele da Como OFM. Conry is saying 'Expers Mendae' ('without fault or blemish'). The words above his head read in English translation: 'Those lambs who are near he teaches by example; those afar off by his writings.' In the background hangs a portrait of St Augustine, whose theology Conry championed. (By kind permission of the Order of Franciscans, Dún Mhuire, Killiney.)

Fig. 8 St Anthony's College, Leuven, was founded by Florence
Conry in 1607. It quickly became the most important Irish
Franciscan college and played a pivotal role in the reorganisation of
the Irish Church, in Gaelic scholarship and in seventeenth-century
Irish politics. (© Museum Leuven.)

Fig. 9 The Cloth Hall, Leuven. From 1432, when Leuven University received permission to establish a faculty of theology, it rented space in the former municipal cloth hall. In 1679 the university purchased the hall. A great number of Irish students attended class in this building, and some, such as John Sinnich of Cork (1603–66), lectured there. This is an engraving from 1610. (Universiteitsarchief, Katholieke Universiteit Leuven.)

Fig. 10 St Isidore's College, Rome. In 1625 Luke Wadding was asked to take over the running of a partially built Franciscan house in the city of Rome. He accepted the charge on condition that the building, once completed, would house a college for the Irish Franciscans. This became St Isidore's. The chapel is embellished with work by Bernini, Maratta and others. (Courtesy of Collegio S. Isidoro, Rome.)

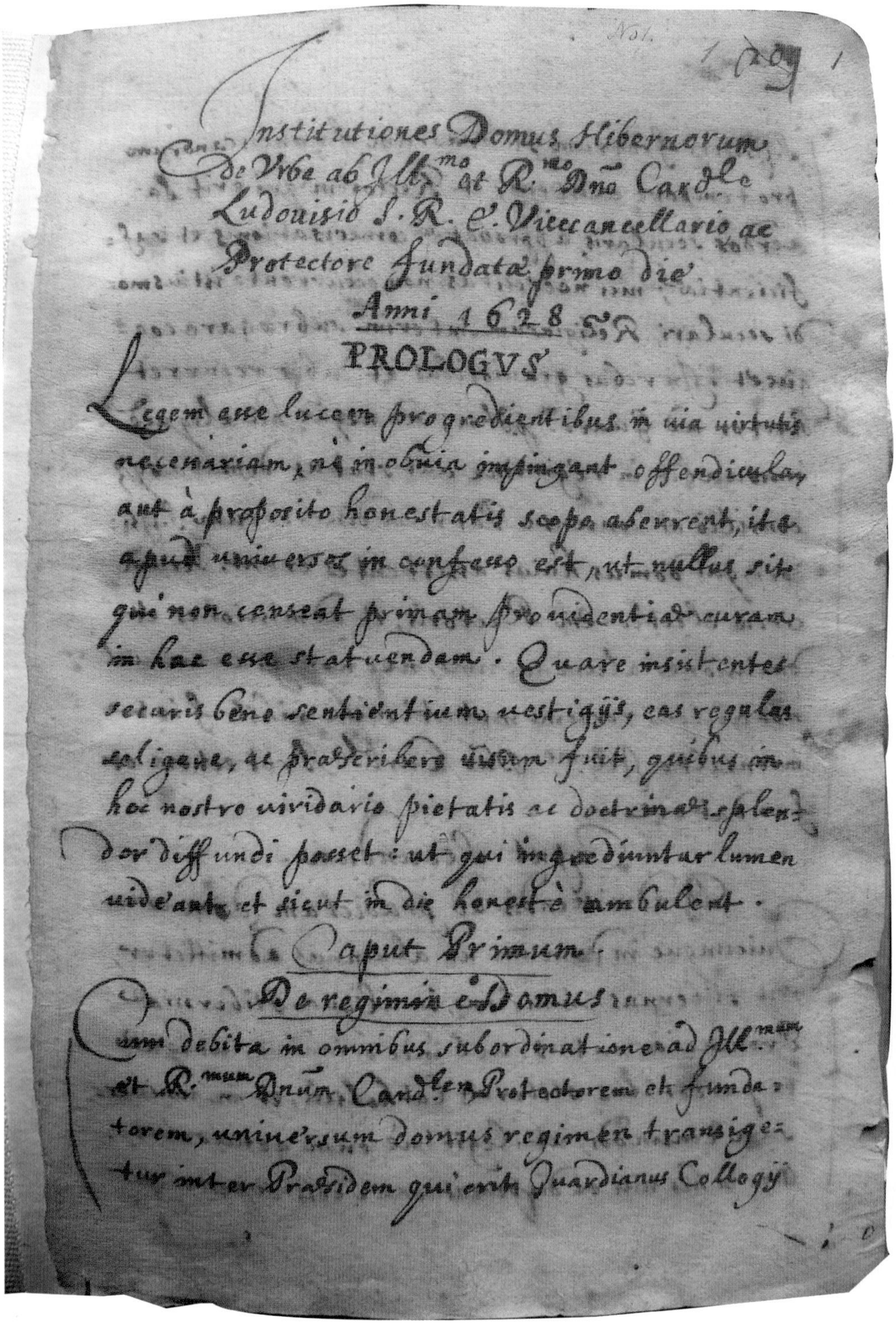
Institutiones Domus Hibernorum
de Urbe ab Ill.mo et R.mo D.no Card.le
Ludovisio S.R.E. Vicecancellario ac
Protectore fundatae primo die
Anni 1628
PROLOGUS
Legem esse lucem progredientibus in via virtutis necessariam, ne in obvia impingant offendicula, aut à proposito honestatis scopo aberrent, ita apud universos in confesso est, ut nullus sit qui non censeat primam providentiae curam in hac esse statuendam. Quare insistentes sectaris bene sentientium vestigiis, eas regulas colligere, ac praescribere visum fuit, quibus in hoc nostro viridario pietatis ac doctrinae splendor diffundi posset: ut qui ingrediuntur lumen videant, et sicut in die honestè ambulent.
Caput Primum
De regimine Domus
Cum debita in omnibus subordinatione ad Ill.mum et R.mum D.num Card.lem Protectorem et fundatorem, universum domus regimen transigetur inter Praesidem qui erit Guardianus Collegii

Fig. 11 Irish college, Rome, foundation document (1628). The Irish pastoral college, Rome, opened its doors in early 1628, thanks to the generosity of the nephew of Pope Gregory XV, Cardinal Ludovico Ludovisi. He was the cardinal-protector of Ireland. Luke Wadding OFM, who had recently founded the Franciscan college of St Isidore's in the city, was put in charge of the new institution, which had about half a dozen students. The first rector was Fr Eugene Callanan, a priest of the diocese of Killaloe. In 1635 the college came under Jesuit control, and students attended classes in the Collegio Romano, also run by the Society of Jesus. This document is a copy of the first page of the college constitutions, drawn up at the time of foundation. (Institutiones domus Hibernorum de Urbe, Archives of the Pontifical Irish College, Rome, Lib 27, fol. 1r.)

Fig. 12 Luke Wadding (1588–1657), Franciscan priest, historian and champion of Scotism, was a native of Waterford and was educated in Portugal and Spain. He travelled to Rome in the late 1610s and resided in San Pietro in Montorio. In 1625 he founded the Irish Franciscan college of St Isidore and two years later was instrumental in the founding of the Irish pastoral college in the city. He was one of the leading Irish intellectual figures of the seventeenth century. (By kind permission of the Order of Franciscans, Dún Mhuire, Killiney.)

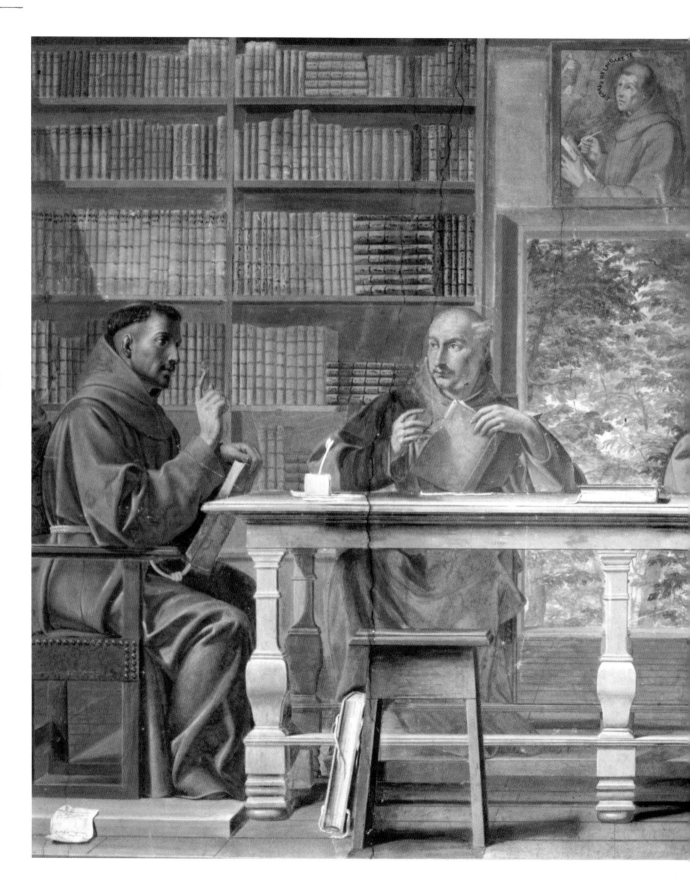

Fig. 13 Groups of scholarly Franciscans, Rome. Under Luke Wadding and his successors, St Isidore's functioned as a centre of intellectual activity, particularly with regard to the history of the Franciscan order and Scotism. In this group by Emanuele da Como OFM, Wadding is last figure on the right. (By kind permission of the Order of Franciscans, Dún Mhuire, Killiney.)

Fig. 14 Thomas Fleming (1591/2–1651), Catholic archbishop of Dublin, was probably born at Slane Castle, Co. Meath. He entered the Irish Franciscans in Leuven in 1612, became guardian and, in 1623, was appointed to Dublin. He was involved in several disputes with clergy in the city. Influential during the Confederate Wars in the 1640s, he died during the Siege of Galway. (By kind permission of the Order of Franciscans, Dún Mhuire, Killiney.)

Fig. 15 Maurice a Portu O'Fihelly (d. 1516), a native of Clonfert diocese, travelled to Italy in the 1480s and entered the School of Franciscan Studies in Milan. He held the chair of Scotist philosophy at Padua University from 1494 to 1513. In 1506 he was appointed archbishop of Tuam but did not return home until 1513. He was an accomplished Scotist and was known as 'Flos Mundi'. (By kind permission of the Order of Franciscans, Dún Mhuire, Killiney.)

Fig. 16 John Punch (1599–1672/3) was born in Cork. He joined the Irish Franciscan college in Leuven, studied philosophy at Cologne and then moved to the Franciscan college in Rome. By 1630 he was rector there and he later became governor of the Irish pastoral college in the city. From 1634 he assisted Wadding in producing the first complete edition of the works of John Duns Scotus. Punch was a central figure in the revival and development of Scotism. (By kind permission of the Order of Franciscans, Dún Mhuire, Killiney.)

Fig. 17 Duns Scotus (*c.* **1265–1308), Franciscan friar and theologian**, was born in Scotland, but in the seventeenth century many Irish Franciscans believed he was Irish. Scotus developed a scholastic system of thought known as Scotism, which the Irish Franciscans championed. In 1639 an edition of his works was published by Luke Wadding. Scotus was known as the Subtle Doctor. This portrait is in St Isidore's, Rome. (By kind permission of the Order of Franciscans, Dún Mhuire, Killiney.)

Ansicht des Hiberner Plazes gegen die Pflaster Gasse.   *Vue de la Place des Irlandois vers la Rue pavée.*

Dedie à Son Excellence Monsieur Jean François   *Comte de Sweertz et Spork, Baron de Reist,*

Seigneur de Liffa, Schlüsselbourg, et Pronogee, &c. &c.   *Conseiller intime de sa Majesté Impériale Royale et Apostol.*

Fig. 18 Irish Franciscan college, Prague. The Irish Franciscans founded two successful colleges in Leuven (1607) and Rome (1625) but quickly felt the need for new accommodation. In the late 1620s they were invited by the archbishop of Prague to found a college in his diocese. This eighteenth-century engraving features the church of the Franciscan college. John Toland visited the college and was impressed by the kind reception he received. The college was closed in 1786 by Joseph II as part of his plans for rationalising religion in his dominions. Portions of its library were integrated into other collections in Prague, Olomouc and elsewhere in Bohemia, where they survive to this day. (The City of Prague Museum.)

Fig. 20 Irish pastoral college, Leuven (Pencil drawing, end 18th century). The Irish pastoral college in Leuven was founded in 1624 by Eugene MacMahon, archbishop of Dublin and native of the diocese of Clogher. It was supported by grants from the Irish Catholic bishops, the archbishop of Malines (Brussels) and the Congregation of Propaganda Fide in Rome. Its early years were marked by controversy. It survived until the late 1790s. (Katholieke Universiteit Leuven, University Library, Print Room)

Fig. 19 Irish Dominican convent at Leuven (Lithograph after an 18th century drawing in E. van Even, Louvain Monumental, Leuven, 1860). Like other religious orders in Ireland, the Dominicans lost their Irish properties during the Reformation. By the end of the sixteenth century, however, they were reorganising. Later, in the mid-1620s, they founded a college in Leuven, the first superior of which was Dominic O'Daly OP (1595–1662). It closed during the French Revolutionary Wars in the late 1790s. The building that housed the community was destroyed during the Second World War. (Katholieke Universiteit Leuven, University Library, Print Room)

42

78

Fig. 21 (b) Theology theses completed by Irish students in Paris in the 1640s. A number of Irish theology students in the Sorbonne took advanced degrees in the seventeenth and eighteenth centuries. Degrees were granted after a public presentation or defence of the thesis, a summary of which was published and posted around the university. The student's patron usually paid the publication costs. In the 1640s the Protestant duke of Ormond and his Catholic relations patronised a number of philosophy and theology students, whose theses are reproduced here. (MS Carte 176, fol. 218r; © Bodleian Library, University of Oxford. MS Carte 176, fol. 219r; © Bodleian Library, University of Oxford.)

Fig. 21 (a) Student of the Irish college, Rome. Irish students in the Continental colleges wore distinctive garb, which made them easily identifiable in the streets of Paris, Leuven, Salamanca and Rome. The student in the image wears the formal clerical garb of Irish college students in the eighteenth century. (Filippo Bonanni, *Catalogo degli ordini religiosi…e diversi collegii di alumni, e congregazioni di fanciulle* (4 vols, Rome, 1742; vol. 3, pl. 42).)

Fig. 22 David Rothe (c. 1573–1650) was Catholic bishop of
Ossory from 1618. He appears in this contemporaneous portrait in
ecclesiastical garb. Rothe was educated in the Irish college in
Douai in the 1590s and travelled to Spain and Rome. He returned
to Ireland in 1609. Rothe was a prolific writer, a keen historian
and a committed pastor. (Private collection.)

Bishop Thomas Dease   1568 – 1652 –
BISHOP OF MEATH 1622 – 165?

Fig. 23 Thomas Dease (1568–1652), a native of Westmeath, was educated in the Irish college, Douai. He moved to Paris, where he became second rector of the Irish college there. A noted canonist, he was appointed bishop of Meath in 1621. He was an accomplished Irish-language poet and an important figure in the Catholic revival of the early seventeenth century. His loyalist stance in the Confederate Wars caused controversy. He died during the Siege of Galway. (Courtesy of Cathedral House, Mullingar.)

81

Fig. 24 Cornelius Nary (1658–1738). Nary was born in Kildare in 1658 and was ordained a priest in Kilkenny in 1682. He went to Paris and lived in the Collège des Lombards, which housed the Irish college. After a short spell in London, he returned to Dublin in 1699 and became parish priest of St Michan's. He was a noted controversialist, publishing *A modest and true account of the chief points in controversy between Roman Catholics and Protestants* in 1696, and in 1724 he wrote *The case of the Roman Catholics of Ireland*, which argued against the Penal Laws. In 1720 he published *A new history of the world.* (National Library of Ireland, Prints and Drawings Collection.)

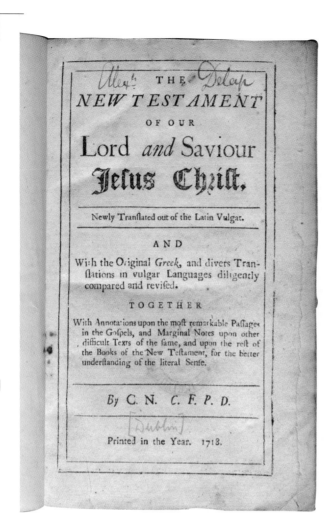

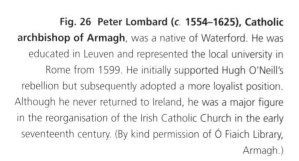

THE
NEW TESTAMENT
OF OUR
Lord *and* Saviour
Jesus Christ.

Newly Translated out of the Latin Vulgat.

AND

With the Original *Greek*, and divers Tran-
slations in vulgar Languages diligently
compared and revised.

TOGETHER

With Annotations upon the most remarkable Passages
in the Gospels, and Marginal Notes upon other
difficult Texts of the same, and upon the rest of
the Books of the New Testament, for the better
understanding of the literal Sense.

By C. N. C. F. P. D.

[Dublin]

Printed in the Year. 1718.

Fig. 25 Cornelius Nary's *New Testament*. In 1715 Nary completed his translation into English of the New Testament. It caused him trouble in Rome, where his interest in the vernacular was interpreted as sympathy for dissident movements in the Church associated with the second, political phase of Jansenism.

Fig. 26 Peter Lombard (c. 1554–1625), Catholic archbishop of Armagh, was a native of Waterford. He was educated in Leuven and represented the local university in Rome from 1599. He initially supported Hugh O'Neill's rebellion but subsequently adopted a more loyalist position. Although he never returned to Ireland, he was a major figure in the reorganisation of the Irish Catholic Church in the early seventeenth century. (By kind permission of Ó Fiaich Library, Armagh.)

Fig. 27 Peter Talbot (1620–80). This mid-seventeenth-century oil painting of Peter Talbot, Catholic archbishop of Dublin from 1669, captures something of his confidence and tenacity. A native of Dublin, he was educated in Lisbon, where he joined the Jesuits. He was an accomplished linguist and an able public man, but his political intrigues, domestic and international, earned him the enmity of many. (Courtesy of the National Gallery of Ireland; photo © The National Gallery of Ireland.)

Fig. 28 Daniel O'Connell (1775–1847), Irish national figure, had an uncle who was lieutenant-general in the service of Louis XVI and, from 1783, a count of France. Like many of his countrymen, O'Connell spent a spell in Europe. In 1791 he travelled to the Austrian Netherlands and entered the English college in St Omer, where he spent a year. The Revolutionary Wars forced him to seek refuge in London in 1793. A good number of the Catholic elite in Ireland benefited from longer or shorter stays on the Continent. (Courtesy of the National Gallery of Ireland; photo © The National Gallery of Ireland.)

Fig. 29 Abbess Lady Joseph Butler (1641–1723), a cousin of the Protestant duke of Ormond, was
one of the many Irishwomen who left Ireland for religious reasons. She travelled to Ypres and joined
the Benedictine house there, later becoming the community's first Irish abbess. In 1688 the Catholic
James II invited her to Dublin to found a house. After the Battle of the Boyne, she returned to Ypres.
For the next five years she lived with just four nuns in poverty and was advised to dissolve the
monastery. She decided to persevere, and the community lived on. She died in 1723. (Courtesy of
Kylemore Abbey.)

Fig. 30 Façade of the Abbey of Irish Dames, Ypres. The Irish Benedictine community that lived in this house was founded by Lady Marina Beaumont (1665–82). It was intended for exiled Irishwomen with religious vocations. Under its first Irish abbess, Lady Joseph Butler, the community moved briefly to Ireland. It endured mixed fortunes until the First World War forced it to transfer to England, later to Wexford and finally to its present location in Kylemore Abbey, Co. Galway. (Patrick Nolan, *The Irish Dames of Ypres; being a history of the Royal Irish Abbey at Ypres founded 1665 and still flourishing* (Dublin, 1908).)

| 85

Fig. 31 St Patrick's College, Maynooth (1801). The French Revolutionary Wars of the 1790s led to the closure of Irish colleges in France, Spain, Flanders and Italy. The ensuing shortage of priests provoked a pastoral crisis in Ireland. In 1795 the Catholic bishops, with the help of the Dublin government and the reluctant cooperation of the Protestant Dublin parliament, founded the Royal Catholic College of St Patrick at Maynooth to produce priests domestically. This watercolour shows the college from the east, with the original Stoyte House, home of the land steward of the dukes of Leinster, already flanked by student accommodation, the unimaginatively named 'Long Corridor'. The impressive ruins of Maynooth Castle, original home of the FitzGerald earls of Kildare, are on the right-hand side of the image. It features a more modern dwelling-house, since removed. (Courtesy of St Patrick's College, Maynooth.)

Fig. 32 Thomas Hussey (1746–1803), first president of Maynooth College and bishop of Waterford, was a native of Ballinabrackey, Co. Meath. He was educated in the Irish college in Seville and acted as chaplain in the Spanish embassy in London. Hussey was a key figure in the Irish Catholic Church's efforts to adjust to the closure of the Continental colleges and to closer cooperation with the London and Dublin governments. He was associated with the family of Edmund Bourke, great friends of Maynooth. Hussey was a strong advocate of freedom of religious practice for Catholic soldiers in royal service in Ireland. In this portrait he holds the plans for Maynooth College. (Courtesy of St Patrick's College, Maynooth.)

Fig. 33 Irish college, Paris, entrance. The Irish student community in Paris dates from the 1570s, but it was only in the early seventeenth century that it acquired a residence. During the following half-century it changed location frequently before occupying the Collège des Lombards on the rue des Carmes in the 1670s. A century later part of the Irish student community moved into new premises designed by François-Joseph Bélanger (1744–1818). The entrance of the new building, pictured here, features the harp and the crown of Ireland. (Photo: Gerard Long, 2007.)

Fig. 34 Irish college, Paris, courtyard. The scale and quality of the new Irish college in the rue du Cheval Vert, opened in 1776, were testimony to the improved circumstances of the Irish ecclesiastical community abroad. Bélanger's design, influenced by Ledroux, consisted of a fifteen-bay, four-storey façade with wings on the garden front. During the Second Empire, additions were made and much of the interior decoration was changed. (Photo: Gerard Long, 2007.)

 | 87

Fig. 35 Irish college, Rome. Thanks to the generosity of Cardinal Ludovico Ludovisi, protector of Ireland, and Luke Wadding OFM, the Irish pastoral college was founded in 1627. It came under Jesuit control in 1633. Its roll-call of the famous included St Oliver Plunkett (1625–81). The present building, designed by Giuseppe Momo and pictured here, dates from the 1920s. (Photo: Rev. Albert McDonnell, 2007.)

Fig. 36 Rector's desk, Irish college, Salamanca. The Irish college in Salamanca was founded in 1592 by Thomas White with a grant from King Philip II. It was run by the Irish Jesuits and became the most important of the Irish colleges in Spain. In the 1950s the college was closed, and its library and archive were transported to Maynooth College. The rector's travel desk, pictured here, is preserved in the Russell Library. (Russell Library, National University of Ireland, Maynooth, from the collections of St Patrick's College, Maynooth.)

Fig. 37 St Anthony's College, Leuven, doorway. The doorway to St Anthony's College, Leuven, displays the institution's dedication and features the motto of the Irish Franciscans, 'to the glory of God and the honour of Ireland'. Just beyond the college gate stood the Dutch college, whose president in the late 1610s and early 1620s was Cornelius Jansen (1585–1638). He knew and admired Florence Conry, the founder of St Anthony's. (Photo: Éilis Ní Dhuibhne, 2007.)

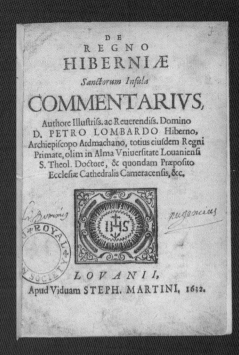

Fig. 38 Peter Lombard's *Commentarius* (1632). Peter Lombard prepared a report on Ireland for Pope Clement VIII in 1600. His intention was to convince the pope to support Hugh O'Neill's rebellion. It argues that O'Neill's rebellion could become the first step in the re-Catholicisation of north-western Europe. Clement was not enthusiastic, and Lombard's own attitude toward O'Neill changed subsequently. A version of Lombard's report was published in Leuven in 1632. The book also contains historical, geographical and economic material on late sixteenth-century Ireland.

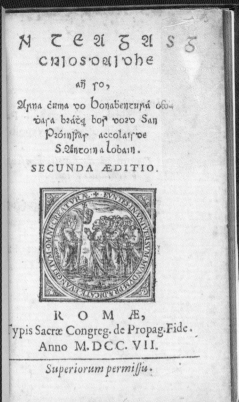

Fig. 39 Giolla Brighde Ó hEodhasa's catechism. Ó hEodhasa (c. 1570–1614) was born in the diocese of Clogher into a hereditary learned family. He was educated in Flanders, became a Franciscan and taught in St Anthony's. He was the author of *An teagasg Críosdaidhe*, a catechism, which appeared in Antwerp in 1611.

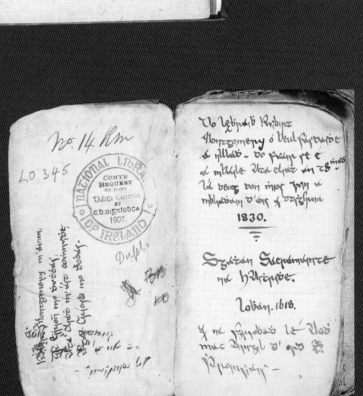

Fig. 40 Aodh Mac Aingil's *Scáthán*. Mac Aingil (1571?–1626), Catholic archbishop of Armagh and theologian, was born in County Down. In 1600 he travelled to Spain, where he attended the University of Salamanca and joined the Franciscans. In 1607 he was appointed to the staff of St Anthony's, Leuven. He composed the devotional work *Scáthán shacramuinte na haithridhe* ('A mirror of the sacrament of penance') in 1618.

SCRIPTORES

ORDINIS MINORVM.

QVIBVS ACCESSIT

SYLLABVS ILLORVM,

qui ex eodem Ordine pro fide Chrifti fortiter occubuerunt.

PRIORES ATRAMENTO, POSTERIORES SANGVINE
CHRISTIANAM RELIGIONEM ASSERVERVNT.

RECENSVIT

FR. LVCAS VVADDINGVS,

eiufdem Inftituti Theologus.

ROMÆ,

Ex Typographia Francifci Alberti Tani. Anno M.DC.L.

SVPERIORVM PERMISSV.

Fig. 41 Luke Wadding's Scriptores. Luke Wadding was an enormously learned figure who excelled as a world-class scholar in many fields. His *Scriptores ordinis minorum,* with a list of martyrs, appeared in 1650. It was one of most important works he wrote in defence of the Franciscan order.

FOCALÓIR

GAOIDHILGE-

SAX-BHÉARLA

OR,

AN IRISH-ENGLISH DICTIONARY.

A

His, her. ex. *a cheann*, his head, *a ceann*, her head.

A their. ex. *a cceann*, their chief, or, their head. *a cclann*, their Children.

A before inanimate things in the singular number, signifies *its* ex. *a bhun*, its bottom, *a thosach* its beginning.

A is a sign of the present & preter tenses. ex. *a deir mé*, J say, *a dùbhairt sé*, he said.

A is sometimes a sign of the future tense. ex *an àit as a ttiocfadh sé*. the place from which he shall come.

A is a sign of the vocative case, and signifies the same as *tu* or *o* in Latin. ex. *a Dhia* o God *a Dhuine*, you man, or o man.

A

42 John O'Brien's dictionary. John O'Brien (Séan Ó Briain) (1701–69), ... tholic bishop of Cloyne and Ross and lexicographer, was a native of Cork. ... was educated in Toulouse and returned to Ireland in 1738. His greatest ... ork was as general editor of an Irish dictionary, *Focalóir Gaoidhilge– ...x-Bhéarla*, compiled by other scholars under his supervision before 1762 and ...entually printed at Paris in 1768.

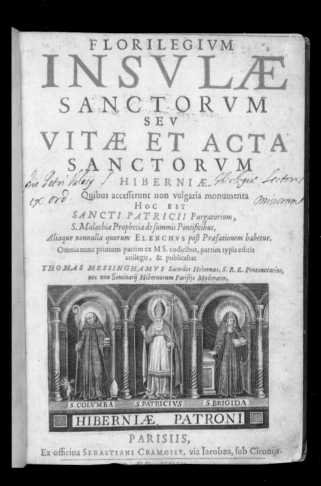

Fig. 43 Thomas Messingham's *Florilegium insulae sanctorum* (1624). The seventeenth century saw a revival in interest in Irish history and the Irish saints. Thomas Messingham's work, published in Paris in 1624, was a compilation of texts, ancient and contemporary, dealing with the principal patrons of Ireland. Messingham himself executed the drawings on which the engravings featured here were based.

91

4. Trading places: Irish merchant communities in Europe

Merchants played a vital role in maintaining Ireland's connection with continental Europe throughout the late medieval and early modern eras, facilitating constant transfer of goods, passengers, news and ideas. In the sixteenth century, Ireland's strongest commercial links were with England, Flanders, the Iberian peninsula and France, with merchant families in the southern ports of Waterford and Cork having particularly close ties with France and northern Spain. In the early 1600s Ireland's economy was very underdeveloped by Continental standards, and Irish export commodities consisted almost exclusively of agricultural produce—hides, friezes (coarse woollen cloths), salted beef, cattle, sheep, canvases, wool, yarn, rugs, tallow, candles, butter and fish. While the most popular imports remained wine, salt, iron, corn and dye stuffs, both Irish and European merchants strove to meet the growing demand in Ireland for luxury commodities including honey, liquorice, soap, tobacco, sugar, books and even stained glass and fabrics such as silk.

The genesis of Irish merchant communities in Europe

Up until the 1630s, although a small number of Irish merchants resided in ports such as Bordeaux, Nantes, Saint-Malo, Dieppe and La Coruña, there were no significant Irish merchant communities *per se* in Europe. In the early 1600s many Irish merchants continued to operate as seafarers, anchoring in several ports in the course of a round trip and finding lodgings in the private houses of native merchants or in the local hostelries, where they conversed, gambled and drank with English merchants and mariners. Typically, they spent several weeks in each port, bargaining, chartering and loading ships for their return trip home. Others preferred to operate from their base in Ireland, enlisting the services of relatives resident in Continental ports to act on their behalf.

Paving the way

From the late sixteenth century, individual merchants

from major ports in Ireland, many of them from the ranks of the Old English elite, settled in Iberia and France. A branch of the Comerford family from Waterford resided in La Coruña, the most important port in the north-west of Spain. 'Roberto Comorforte y Compañía' operated in partnership with his brothers Jorge, Jaime and Patrique, his cousin Guillermo Comorforte and Juonis Fagan, all of them citizens of Waterford. Like most Irish merchants abroad, Robert concentrated on trade with Ireland, and he became one of the wealthiest merchants in La Coruña. Similarly, in Saint-Malo members of the Lynch, Kirwan and French families of Galway played a vital role in maintaining a lively trade between these two ports in the early decades of the seventeenth century, overseeing all stages in transactions from sourcing commodities to charting and loading ships destined for Galway.

Despite their modest number, these merchants fulfilled several important functions within the wider Irish émigré population on the Continent, as can be seen in the career of Robert Comerford. He played a significant role as intermediary between the Old English merchants and clerics and the Galician regional and military government. He served as consul of the merchants from Scotland, Ireland, the Holy Roman Empire and Flanders in the first quarter of the seventeenth century. He also operated within a network of financiers who supplied loans to individuals and who employed members of other Old English families. As one of his sons, Juan, was a student at the Irish seminary in Alcalá in the early 1600s, Robert paid fees of between 600 and 800 reales per annum for Juan's maintenance during his studies and subsequently continued to make generous contributions towards the upkeep of the cash-starved college.

Many of these early settlers quickly integrated into their host society, some through marriage, others through acquisition of office. Within the space of approximately fifteen years, Robert Comerford's family had become so thoroughly integrated that after

1600 they were identified no longer as Irish but as citizens of La Coruña. That process advanced in the next generation, as two of his daughters married Spaniards. Further proof of the high esteem in which Robert was held by the upper echelons of La Coruña society came with their appointment of his son Jorge to succeed him in the prestigious office of consul. The same pattern is evident in Breton ports: in Saint-Malo, for instance, by the mid-1620s the Galway merchant Simon Lynch was sufficiently integrated into Malouin society to secure the post of town burgher.

Setting down roots

From the 1630s the phenomenon of transient Irish merchants was becoming a thing of the past, as mounting economic and religious pressures in Ireland caused growing numbers of Catholic merchants to transfer their business to ports on the Continent, such as La Rochelle, Saint-Malo and Nantes, where they already had family and commercial contacts. These embryonic Irish merchant communities expanded during the 1640s with the influx of additional merchants owing to civil war at home. However, their numbers swelled much more dramatically in the 1650s, when the entire Catholic merchant class of Waterford, along with many more from Wexford and other ports, relocated to French, Spanish and Flemish ports. They did so largely to escape the Cromwellian regime, but undoubtedly they were also driven by a desire to capitalise on the flourishing overseas trade of the Atlantic ports. Several factors smoothed the way for their speedy integration into the commercial spheres of their adoptive cities and towns. In France the king's abhorrence at the regicide in England and the usurpation of government by Oliver Cromwell was reflected in his orders to all officials to 'favoriser les Catholiques Irlandais en tout ce que dépendra de nous' ('support the Irish Catholics in all that will depend on us'). In Spain, since the early 1600s, the Irish had used their control over the post of consul in various coastal ports throughout Andalusia to extract privileges from the Spanish monarch. This laid the basis for their commercial prosperity in the next century. The Southern Netherlands also emerged as an attractive destination, especially for Waterford and Wexford merchant families, many of whom settled in the burgeoning maritime trading centre of Ostend and also in Bruges. At that time the Southern Netherlands was the economic heart of Europe, surrounded by the booming Atlantic economies of England, the Dutch Republic and France, and thus provided entrepreneurs such as the Carews and Lynches of Waterford with a gateway to a wider variety of business ventures than they could ever have hoped for back in Ireland.

Consolidating foundations for empire-building

Having settled abroad, these Irish merchants typically maintained close connections with their native ports while progressively integrating Ireland into a wider, thriving Continental commercial network that extended to penetrate the Spanish, French and Dutch overseas empires in the Americas and India.

The 1670s witnessed a further resurgence in merchant migration from Ireland, notably from the ports of Waterford, Limerick and Galway. For all those who transferred their businesses abroad in the middle decades of the seventeenth century, making the requisite legal provisions to secure their commercial and private assets, along with inheritance rights, was a major priority. As naturalisation was typically a long-drawn-out process, many initiated proceedings to become naturalised citizens immediately after their arrival. In Brittany this resurgence resulted in growing numbers of naturalisations, from an average of one per four or five years before the 1670s to an average of one per year after 1676.

Entrepreneurs and emerging empires

After the deposition of James II in 1689 and the subsequent introduction of the Penal Laws, a wave of Irish merchant émigrés, the vast majority of them Catholic and armed with considerable capital,

commercial aspirations and entrepreneurial skills, left Ireland intent on setting up business in a more congenial milieu abroad. The majority settled in ports with existing Irish merchant communities: strong entrepreneurial families such as the MacNemaras and O'Shiels settled in Nantes, and in Ostend the ranks of the tiny Irish merchant community swelled significantly with the arrival of Fitzgeralds, Porters, Archdeacons and Rays. Others preferred to settle in new locations: Francis Jennings from Belfast settled in Sweden and became a leader in the export of Stockholm iron by the 1720s.

The Irish invested their capital as a step towards the formation of a commercial base abroad. Their rapid integration into more far-flung Jacobite commercial networks was assisted by the dispersal of large numbers of their compatriots across many European ports. Consequently, right from the time that they arrived on the Continent, these émigré merchants were operating within a network of busy ports across western Europe (including Ireland), the Americas and the East Indies. In short, they became quickly immersed in the eighteenth-century globalisation of European economic activity.

Getting started: Irish networking in Ostend

Between 1694 and 1706, a mixed group of young Irish merchants and mariners arrived in the Southern Netherlands, the most notable being Matthew Prosser, Fitzgerald and Matthew Porter, all from Waterford, William Archdeacon from Cork and Thomas Ray (O'Regan) from Youghal. Their career trajectories highlight the lucrative commercial opportunities that were on offer to such enterprising émigrés. Operating from Bruges, Prosser imported hides, butter and soot from Ireland and built up a network of customers in northern France and the Low Countries. After 1715 he imported snuff from Spain and specialised in importing tobacco from the West Indies. By marrying his daughter to Endymion Porter, the manager of a firm in Cádiz, Prosser founded the highly successful house of Prosser

& Porter, which subsequently invested in the Ostend East India trade. Fitzgerald belonged to a very influential family that ran a leading firm in London and oversaw a wide range of commercial activities for a network of Irish merchants across Europe during the first half of the eighteenth century. He focused mainly on shipping wine and salt between Bordeaux and Nantes. Soon after his arrival in 1694 Matthew Porter began operating out of Bruges, concentrating on trade with Ireland, northern France, Holland, London and Iberia. He used his connections with the Prossers to extend his network to Cádiz. Like Matthew Porter, William Archdeacon first migrated to Ostend, in 1705, but he subsequently settled in Bruges, where he played a prominent role in the commercial life of the city. Working in partnership with his uncle, Henry Archdeacon, who was based in Cork, William provided Henry's customers in Antwerp, Brussels and Namur with hides from Cork, Limerick and Dublin. He capitalised on his family connections in Cádiz to purchase salt and West Indian hides in Spain and commissioned the Irish firm of Carew, Langton & Company to act as his agent for trade with the Indies and America. At the end of his career (1755), Archdeacon regarded himself as the main importer of salt to the Southern Netherlands.

However, by far the most successful of this generation of Irish merchants was Thomas Ray. Like several émigré privateers from Waterford and Wexford, Ray engaged in the risky privateering business off the French–Flemish coast as a sideline. By chartering Flemish ships on behalf of Irish merchants in Cádiz and Seville, he facilitated their trade with Ireland. He also used his connections with a Waterford-born merchant, Edward Gough, in Cádiz to build up his own Iberian trade after the mid-1710s. By then Ray was recognised by his peers in Ostend as 'een man van seer grote affaires' ('a big businessman') and had emerged as a pioneer of the East India trade organised in the Southern Netherlands. He subsequently acted more or less as a godfather to several young Irish merchants in

Ostend, admitting them to his merchant house in order to learn about the business and providing them with opportunities to earn handsome profits through trading with the Ostend Company. By the early 1720s Ray was one of a handful of millionaires living in the Southern Netherlands, and he was certainly the richest man in Ostend.

This colony of Irish merchants and entrepreneurs dominated Ostend's international maritime trade during the years 1715–35. However, after the middle of the eighteenth century that Irish influence declined dramatically as fewer Irish merchants were attracted by the prospect of participating in the East India ventures. Leading merchant families such as the Archdeacons and Leys had moved to Bruges, and subsequently only the Rays and Hennessys were left to maintain the Irish mercantile connection in Ostend.

Quays of the empire: the Irish in Spain

In the early decades of the eighteenth century Irish merchants trading in ports throughout Spain and the Canary Islands were especially adept at capitalising on their Catholicism and they used their special relationship with the Spanish Crown to be granted Spanish nationality, a prerequisite for trading with the New World. Their privileged status was copper-fastened in 1759 by a royal decree that conferred on Irish Catholics who had lived in Spain for more than ten years or who had married a Spaniard the right to trade freely and to own property. The Irish also benefited from successive Anglo-Spanish crises during the eighteenth century, which disrupted the British mercantile communities in Spain and the Canary Islands. When the War of the Spanish Succession (1701–14) forced English businessmen in the Canaries and Cádiz to leave, during their absence smaller Irish houses took over their trade, and after the war ended the Irish more than held their own in the market, progressively becoming the largest foreign group in the Canaries and emerging to dominate trade with England in Cádiz. Interestingly, when Protestant merchants returned in 1713 and found themselves at a disadvantage, it was leading Irish Catholics in the business community rather than consuls who made representations on their behalf to the authorities.

Although the ports of Málaga, El Puerto de Santa Maria, Huelva, Seville, Cartagena, La Coruña, Rota, Sanlúcar de Barrameda and the Canary Islands were popular Spanish destinations for Irish merchants in the 1690s and early 1700s, none rivalled Cádiz. After that port assumed the monopoly on trade with the Indies in 1717, it enjoyed a period of unprecedented commercial prosperity, and a small number of Irish merchant families, notably Cologans, Walshes, Ryans, Terrys, O'Crouleys, Flemings, Leys, Carews and Murphys, played a significant part in that commercial success story. Interestingly, the founders of the city's merchant population included a sizeable Jacobite gentry element, who evidently made a calculated commercial decision to redirect their business acumen and capital into developing trade connections with the Spanish overseas territories. The Irish presence grew dramatically over the century, from 21 families in 1709 to 128 in 1791, but the community went into decline after the Battle of Trafalgar (1805).

The family was the fundamental unit in all Irish merchant communities, and strategic marriage alliances were therefore vital for strengthening their business interests. Among first-generation merchants, in particular, endogamy was the norm, and many marriages between partners living in different cities or countries were contracted by proxy. For example, in 1700 Bernard Walsh, one of Tenerife's leading Irish merchants, formed a partnership with George Fitzgerald, a member of a Waterford family with trading connections in Nantes and Saint-Malo. Four years later Walsh married George's niece, Francisca-Xaviera Geraldine, the daughter of a merchant in Nantes. The couple's daughters married into the Gough family of Cádiz, the Quilty family of Málaga and the leading merchant family in the Canaries, the Cologans. These carefully arranged marriages secured succession

lines and guaranteed retention of the business within a family, as well as bringing in new partners and capital (especially dowries) and extending commercial networks across Europe and throughout the overseas empires. In order to consolidate their commercial interests in the Americas, Irish merchants dispatched their sons to Mexico and elsewhere to acquire experience and establish contacts.

In mid-eighteenth-century Cádiz the Irish merchant community was a thriving trading hub within an international commercial network. One of its most successful companies, founded by Lawrence Carew, had connections with Ostend, London, Genoa, Lisbon and Barcelona, along with more far-flung destinations including Veracruz in Mexico and Cartagena de Indias, and when Carew died in 1766 his assets were valued at over two million pesos.

The ranks of Irish merchant communities in Cádiz, Alicante and Seville were swelled by the arrival of a second generation of Irish houses from France on either side of 1750. At that time these communities ranked third after the French and Spanish in terms of their income. Even the most successful Irish merchants were usually more interested in acquiring noble titles and investing their profits in land and property than in accumulating capital. Above all, they were determined to consolidate their position by securing legal recognition of their noble status (*hidalguía*) and by participating fully in the civic life of their host society.

The cases of William Terry (1726–79) of El Puerto de Santa Maria, near Cádiz, and Pedro Alonso O'Crouley (1740–1817) of Cádiz provide vignettes of the privileged lifestyles but also the priorities of the most successful Irish merchant houses in southern Spain in the mid-eighteenth century. The Terrys were among the Jacobite émigrés who settled in Cádiz; over three generations the family built up a substantial commercial enterprise, based mainly on trade with the Americas, and in 1760 they owned three ships. By then William Terry was head of the family. He inherited the Spanish noble titles of *marqués* and *caballero de Santiago* and pursued a high-profile public career as *alférez mayor*, or royal representative in council affairs. While his family's merchant business continued to thrive, he purchased several farms on which he grew vines and olives. William was fluent in English, Latin, Italian and French, and in his household in El Puerto he had on a display a magnificent collection of antique medallions. He and his family lived in a comfortable home staffed by a butler, a page, a cook, a cook's help, a housekeeper, a wet nurse, four maids and a special maid to attend on his wife, Maria Francisca Lacy, who was of Irish descent and who had formerly served as lady-in-waiting to Queen Maria de Palma. A Turkish slave named Maria Madalena also resided in the Terry household. Pedro Alonso O'Crouley was head of another highly successful Irish merchant family in Cádiz. As a youth, like many merchants' sons, he spent time in Mexico, learning his family trade before returning to Cádiz in 1774. Educated in Senlis in France and a member of several learned societies, Pedro Alonso spent his family's fortune very conspicuously on a renowned collection of coins, medallions and over 200 paintings, which included works by Rubens, Van Dyke and Velázquez. He and his wife, Mary Power, who was of Irish descent, lived very comfortably with their nine children in a typical eighteenth-century merchant dwelling of three storeys, with stores and offices on the ground floor, the family living quarters on the middle floor, and the kitchen and servants' quarters on the top floor. In 1789, at the age of 49, O'Crouley was conferred with the noble title of *hidalgo*.

The evolution of the Irish merchant community in Málaga followed a similar pattern: early settlement in the city, the establishment and maintenance of a network of relatives in other Andalusian and European ports, an increased number of arrivals from 1730 and the Irish colony outgrowing the rest of the British settlement to become third among foreigners after the Genoese and the French. The Irish were instrumental in integrating their northern European trading partners into networks in the Mediterranean and North Africa.

They traded with Spanish America and maintained frequent contacts with major commercial centres such as Cartagena de Indias, Veracruz and Jalapa. The Irish facilitated the importation to Andalusia and onward transportation to India of woollen fabrics, cotton and linen, trinkets, cod, tanned hides, wheat and manufactured produce. From Andalusia they exported wines, colonial produce and precious metals from America that helped to balance the Spanish budget deficit.

Up until the end of the eighteenth century, economic conditions favoured commercial concerns run by individuals or families in Spain. When the Cádiz monopoly of colonial trade ended in 1778, Irish colonies survived best in satellite ports such as Málaga, a dynamic port with long-established Irish merchant houses that was now able to trade directly to the Americas. However, by the early nineteenth century Irish capital investment began to suffer owing to Spain's wars with England, the opening up of American trade to neutral countries and the deleterious effects of the Napoleonic Wars throughout Europe and in Spain itself.

Vicissitudes of Irish merchant fortunes in France

In the second half of the seventeenth century Saint-Malo and La Rochelle were the leading ports engaged in trade with Ireland. Their Irish merchant communities grew significantly in the 1690s and early 1700s. By then, however, the focal points of Irish commercial development and merchant establishments in France were already shifting to Nantes and Bordeaux, and by 1750 La Rochelle's Irish colony was reduced to just two houses, those of White and Galwey.

A window on the world: Irish merchant houses in Nantes

Nantes was one of the most popular destinations for Jacobite émigrés. In the early decades of the eighteenth century Nantes had strong commercial links with Ireland (in 1714 22 per cent of all ships departing that port were destined for Ireland). The city was home to a thriving Irish community: Thomas and Daniel MacNemara, who had settled there in the 1690s, owned the largest single merchant house, worth 850,000 livres, but the O'Shiels, Shees, Clarkes, Lees, O'Riordans, Browns and Lynches were also generating substantial fortunes. However, from the 1740s the port began to be eclipsed by Bordeaux, largely thanks to the latter's thriving wine export trade and the soaring volume of trade in Irish beef. Many Irish Jacobite families were drawn into colonial trade and investment in overseas plantations, especially in San Domingo (modern Haiti), Martinique, Guadeloupe and Cayenne. One such individual, Barnaby O'Shiel, whose family settled in Nantes, made a substantial fortune from several sugar plantations that he acquired in San Domingo from the mid-1740s onwards. Some Irish Jacobites in Nantes who had ties with houses in Saint-Malo and Lorient established an interest in the Compagnie française des Indies. The fact that several Irish families invested in France's colonial trade at this early stage earned them particular prominence in the city's commercial life.

From the 1640s, when they had begun to settle in the major French Atlantic ports, notably Dunkirk and Saint-Malo but also Nantes, Lorient, La Rochelle, Brest and Bordeaux, the Irish became heavily involved in the highly lucrative business of privateering, piloting ships armed for authorised war against enemies of France. From the 1680s onwards two Irish families, the Walshes and the Geraldines, were especially prominent privateers in Saint-Malo. Antoine Vincent Walsh (1703–63), an ardent Jacobite naval officer turned merchant, became Nantes's leading privateer. It was in one of his vessels that Charles Edward Stuart made the crossing to Scotland in July 1745, only to be defeated at the Battle of Culloden.

During the eighteenth century Nantes was a world leader in the slave trade, and Irish merchants were involved to varying degrees in this trafficking, as were their compatriots in the other major Atlantic ports of Dunkirk, Saint-Malo, Lorient, La Rochelle and Bordeaux. Among these, Antoine Vincent Walsh was especially successful and notorious. Described by contemporaries as tough in business, haughty and difficult, he was ruthless in his pursuit of profit. He overworked his crews, and his practice of overloading ships with slaves caused atrociously high mortality rates. Over a period of twenty years he arranged 46 slave transportation trips, and in 1748 he was involved in establishing the Compagnie de l'Angola, which concentrated on transporting slaves to San Domingo and Martinique. Not surprisingly, Walsh made a substantial fortune from the slave trade, but his prosperity was short-lived, and he died in abject poverty in San Domingo in 1763.

Although Nantes declined as a major Atlantic port, and its previously substantial Irish colony contracted to two or three houses by the 1780s, the full impact of that downturn was offset by Irish families securing their place in the ranks of the French nobility, retiring to the countryside or taking up residence in France's colonies. Thus, most of the Galweys, Stapletons, Riordans, O'Shiels, MacNemaras, Walshes, Gilaghs and Lincolns passed out of active involvement in the city's maritime trade as the decades wore on.

A new vintage: the Irish in Bordeaux

Bordeaux's expanding Irish merchant community reflected the port's thriving Irish trade throughout much of the eighteenth century. In the late 1690s there were only six Irish houses in the city (three of them headed by recently arrived butter merchants) and the colony was smaller than those in La Rochelle, Nantes and Saint-Malo. However, the community underwent remarkable expansion in the period 1715–35 owing to a boom in the wine trade. Rather unusually, several of the most prominent houses established in this era came from regions in Ireland that had no established tradition of mercantile settlement in Continental ports. Bordeaux was also somewhat unusual in that it attracted a number of Protestant families from the north of Ireland (Barton in 1725, Delap in 1736 and Johnston in 1743), as well as from Dublin (the Bradshaws in 1714–25). The sharp rise in Bordeaux's beef trade with Ireland in the late 1730s attracted several Cork and Limerick families whose main interest was in areas other than the wine trade. Most of the major houses were established by mid-century; thereafter the most significant additions were the Dublin Protestant houses of Thomas Gledstanes and the Forster brothers. By the 1770s there existed within the Irish merchant community a tight-knit Protestant coterie comprising the houses of Barton, Delap, Boyd, Skinner, Black, Johnston, Forster and Gledstane. Bonds of religion and specialisation in the wine trade were reinforced by marriage and business partnerships. The Catholic families, who were more numerous and less exclusively reliant on the wine trade, were not so cohesive: only those from Galway (the Lynches, Frenches, Blakes and Kirwans) were related by marriage.

One of the reasons for the success of these Galway families in Bordeaux was the fact that they maintained close commercial contacts with family members operating in the vitally important Dublin market, which consumed two-thirds of the wine shipped to Ireland and roughly half of all wine shipments from Bordeaux to the British Isles. As was the norm, the Irish in Bordeaux had connections with relatives in other Continental ports. The Galweys had ties with the Nantes branch of the family, and John Galwey's son was based in Seville. The Lynches had family members in Cádiz and relatives (the Frenches) in San Sebastián. Families also brought relatives out to train or work in the business.

Unlike their counterparts in Nantes, Irish merchants in Bordeaux did not pass out of the city into country life or into plantation life in the Indies, and, apart from the Quins, no Irish family concentrated on colonial traffic to the exclusion of European and Irish trade. The Irish viewed themselves as a distinct colony and were acutely conscious of their shared interest in protecting their mercantile welfare. The resultant vitality of this colony was reflected in the continual emergence of new

houses in the later decades of the eighteenth century. The strong Galway interest that centred on the Lynches, Kirwans, Frenches and Quins was bolstered mid-century through the establishment of lesser houses by the Blake, Bodkin, Burke, Darcy, Joyce and Mills families. At least 62 Irish surnames appeared in houses or partnerships either opened or operating in the second half of the century.

The remarkable boom that occurred in the brandy trade during the late 1750s and the 1760s encouraged a handful of Irish merchants, the most famous being Richard Hennessy, to set up business in nearby Cognac. Although from 1767 there followed a decade of serious depression in that trade in both Cognac and Bordeaux, in the long run the Irish stake proved extremely significant. In 1766 13,000 cases of cognac were shipped under the Hennessy name; by 1778 this had increased nine-fold.

In the 1770s Bordeaux's Irish merchant community reached its zenith, with three of the city's eight largest houses being Irish. From mid-century the Lawtons were the city's outstanding wine brokers. The Barton, Johnston, Lynch, Gernon, MacCarthy, Boyd, Gledstane, Forster and Kirwan families were all prominent in the wine trade and diversified into ownership of wine chateaux in the Médoc, and many of these Irish wine houses survived beyond the turn of the century.

Although the Irish colony in Bordeaux survived the Revolution quite well, ominous developments gained momentum in the 1780s. For the first time in a century new Irish merchant houses were outnumbered by English ones. Wine consumption in Ireland began to diminish, and the export business consequently contracted. More generally, it was fast becoming evident that Bordeaux's decline within colonial commercial circles was imminent, and hardly an Irish-owned colonial or general trading house survived the storms of the revolutionary and imperial eras. The demise of the closed commercial system that had favoured major ports such as Bordeaux and Cádiz, followed by a major colonial crisis in France from 1791 and in Spain from a decade later, resulted in these two formerly thriving European ports becoming backwaters. However, in both France and Spain, Irish wine houses survived, with those in France proving most successful owing to their larger, more varied and more prestigious wine trade and their strong presence in the London and Irish markets.

Closing accounts

Irish merchant communities, more than any other group of Irish émigrés who settled on the Continent during the seventeenth and eighteenth centuries, were susceptible to external forces bringing sudden and often profound change. Their continued prosperity depended on anticipating and embracing new commercial opportunities further afield, reacting resourcefully to shifts in domestic, Continental and colonial markets, and negotiating impediments such as war and embargos. The unique life cycles of these individual communities in the Southern Netherlands, France and Spain were necessarily contingent upon the fluctuating fortunes of the individual ports in which they operated. However, as in the case of Irish clerical and military communities throughout Europe, the onset of a general decline within Irish merchant communities in ports ranging from Ostend to Bordeaux to Cádiz was evident for years, and in some instances decades, before the outbreak of the French Revolution.

Fig. 1 Principal ports trading with Ireland c. 1600. In addition to transporting cargo between Ireland and the Continent, merchants carried passengers and news, thereby maintaining Ireland's links with Europe. From the early 1600s their trade routes became the major arteries of Irish migration as they conveyed passengers to destinations such as Bristol, Dunkirk, Rouen and La Coruña. During the early 1600s, transit times varied greatly: Waterford to La Rochelle took from six to seventeen days, and Dublin to Holyhead (Wales) took just over a day in summer but two in winter. (Courtesy of Martello Media.)

NORWAY

SWEDEN

GOTHENBURG

DENMARK

DERRY   COLERAINE
DONEGAL
SLIGO   CARRICKFERGUS
DUNDALK
GALWAY   DROGHEDA
IRELAND   DUBLIN HOLYHEAD
LIMERICK   HULL
LIVERPOOL
DINGLE   CHESTER
WATERFORD   HAMBURG
CORK   WEXFORD
KINSALE YOUGHAL   ENGLAND   THE
DUTCH
PROVINCES   POLAND
AMSTERDAM
BRISTOL   ROTTERDAM
PLYMOUTH PORTSMOUTH   DOVER   FLUSHING
CALAIS   OSTEND
DUNKIRK   ANTWERP

LE HARVE   DIEPPE
HARFLEUR
CAEN   HONFLEUR   ROUEN   HOLY ROMAN EMPIRE

ST MALO
QUIMPER   RENNES

NANTES

FRANCE   SWITZERLAND

NORTHERN ITALIAN
STATES

BORDEAUX

SANTIAGO DE
COMPOSTELA
BAYONA   BILBAO   BAYONNE
ST JEAN DE LUZ   PAPAL
STATES

AVIERO
PORTUGAL   SPAIN
ON

SAN LUCAR
DE BARRAMEDA
EL PUERTO
CÁDIZ DE SANTA
MARIA   MÁLAGA

| 101

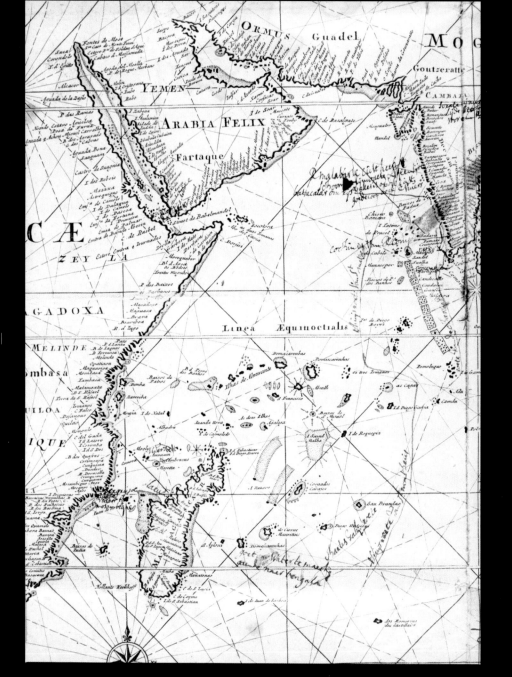

Fig. 2 Detail of a Dutch East India chart. This chart, made by Joannes Loots, c. 1710, was used by Thomas Ray and his captains in 1716 in their preparations for East India voyages. The routes followed by the first two Flemish East India vessels, the *Charles Galleye* and the *Sint-Matteus*, are shown. Because Ray was a director of the Ostend East India Company, several of its ventures received strong Irish financial backing and the logistical organisation of numerous voyages to the east was entrusted to Irish mariners. However, in 1735 the Ostend East India Company was compelled by the major maritime nations to end its commercial activity, although the port continued as an entrepôt for East India commodities. (Rijksarchief Gent/State Archives of Ghent; courtesy of Jan Parmentier.)

Fig. 3 (a and b) Luc O'Shiel (1677–1745), merchant, and his wife Agnès, née Vanasse (1690–1745), of Nantes. In 1689 Luc O'Shiel, the twelve-year-old son of a Dublin merchant, was among the first Irish migrants who left for France after King James II's removal from the throne of England. He settled in Nantes and became a merchant. Having initially traded with Ireland, the Low Countries and Stockholm, after 1706 he concentrated on trade with the West Indies. Like several other Irish merchants in Nantes, O'Shiel became involved in the triangular slave trade between Africa, Europe and the French Caribbean. He became a naturalised French citizen in 1707 and two years later married Agnès. The couple had four children, three of whom married Irish people. (Négociant à Nantes, private collection; courtesy of Patrick Clarke de Dromantin.)

Fig. 4 Le port de Nantes vue du chantier, XVIII siècle. In the eighteenth century, Nantes was a major port in international and European commercial networks. Its geographical location and its history of defending Catholicism made it one of the most important refuges for Irish Jacobites. Welcomed as Catholic refugees, the Irish in Nantes effectively integrated into French society and broadened trade routes from the traditional Nantes–Ireland axis in order to develop a triangular circuit that included the West Indies. (Les Ports de France, Le port de Nantes, vue du chantier de construction de La Fosse, by Nicolas Marie Ozanne (1728–1811) (late eighteenth century), estampe, inv. no. V1b/20043 © Musée national de la Marine.)

Fig. 5 William Archdeacon (1685–1759), his wife, Eleonora Françoise Scharre (d. 1766), and their children (c. 1750). By the 1730s William Archdeacon had established a thriving family business network that connected his native Cork with Rotterdam, Dunkirk, Bruges and Cádiz. In addition to maintaining constant commercial contact with Cork, Archdeacon, like many affluent Irish émigrés, appears to have retained a strong sense of his Irish identity. This is suggested by his playing the harp in this portrait and by his elaborate genealogical pedigree (see Fig. 6). (Private collection, Ghent.)

Fig. 6 Detail of the genealogical pedigree of William Archdeacon of Bruges, eighteenth century. Pedigrees were important for the demonstration of social credentials in *Ancien Régime* Europe. They were vital in cases where displaced individuals and families sought to establish themselves in foreign jurisdictions. Some Irish merchants, having established themselves abroad, enhanced and displayed their economic and social success through the preparation of elaborate pedigrees. (City Archives, Bruges, 531, Genealogies, no. 2.)

**Fig. 7 Panorama of the port of Ostend during the Fourth
Anglo-Dutch War, 1781**. The weakening of the Irish mercantile
presence in Ostend cannot be attributed to a decline in the
economic performance of the Flemish port, which, in fact,
prospered from the 1770s onwards. Competing with Rotterdam
and Dunkirk, Ostend emerged as a major centre for the
distribution of English products on the Continent. Growing
numbers of English merchants became involved in this commercial
enterprise. (Archives of Ostend.)

Fig. 8 Nicholas Porter of Bruges, anonymous, eighteenth century. Many of the leading Irish merchant houses that relocated to the Southern Netherlands, France and Spain were from Waterford. One of the most successful Irish firms in Europe in the early 1700s was half-owned by the family of this man, Nicholas Porter of Bruges. Founded by two Waterford-born merchants, the company Prosser & Porter played a pivotal role in extending the commercial network of Irish merchants in Ostend and Bruges by forging trade links with the thriving port of Cádiz and investing in the Ostend East India Company. (Musea Brugge. Image courtesy of Lukas-Art in Flanders))

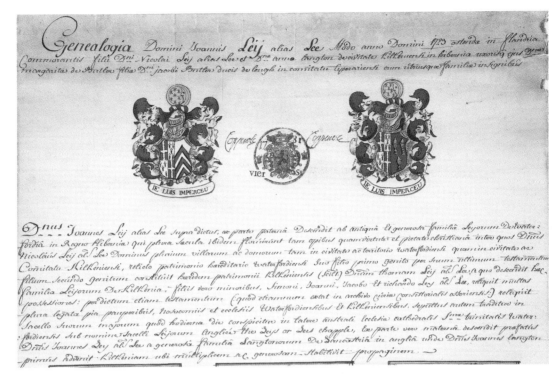

Fig. 9 Detail of the genealogical pedigree of Irish merchant Nicolas Ley of Bruges, eighteenth century. (City Archives, Bruges, Genealogies, no. 25.)

Fig. 10 Manifest of the *Sint-Mattheus* (1716). Announcements of commercial ventures and of the composition of cargoes such as this for the *Sint-Mattheus* were sent to potential investors or clients based in Flanders and Holland. The *Sint-Mattheus* was the first ship to sail from Ostend to the East Indies, in a highly successful venture coordinated by Thomas Ray in 1714–16. The vessel sailed under the command of an Irishman, Xavier Sarsfield, and nine of the ten officers on board originated from Ireland. The enterprise was a great success: one contemporary estimated that it returned a profit of £4000 sterling. However, this stirred the resentment of the rival Dutch and English East India companies, which sought to discredit the 'Ostenders' by circulating stories in Surat that they were, in fact, pirates. (Stadsarchief Antwerpen/City Archives of Antwerp; courtesy of Jan Parmentier.)

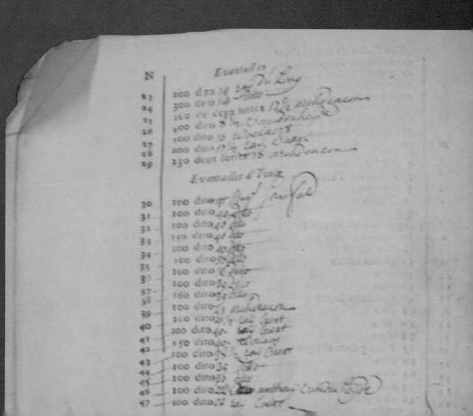

Fig. 11 Letter from Thomas Ray Jnr of Ostend to a relative named Carpentier, 20 February 1758. For all merchants, business and family interests were inextricably intertwined, as this letter illustrates. After the death of Thomas Ray Snr, his son Thomas and his nephew, Patrick Roche, together ran the business. From 1750 they also managed the Ostend merchant house of the immensely wealthy Carpentiers, to whom they were closely related through marriage and for which service they received one-third of all profits. In this letter Thomas Ray Jnr responds to Carpentier's inquiry about shares in Danish vessels and refers to Roche's having been recently diagnosed with epilepsy. (State Archives (Ghent), Algemeen Familiefonds, no. 7719a, 20/02/1758; courtesy of Veerle Delahaye and Jan Parmentier.)

Fig. 12 Extract from an Ostend East India Company auction book (1728). The involvement of several Irish merchant houses in the thriving Ostend East India Company is evidenced by frequent reference to figures including William Archdeacon, Thomas Ray and Patrick Sarsfield in the ledgers of the company's auction books. At the 1728 auction the Irish merchants purchased ivory fans. However, not all Irish involvement with the company was legitimate. During the 1720s and 1730s Patrick Sarsfield, Charles Hennessy and William Archdeacon developed a highly successful system to conceal their smuggling, which was based in Ostend. They purchased Chinese tea and Indian textiles at the public auctions of the Ostend East India Company and then shipped those goods to England, the Isle of Man, the Channel Islands and particularly to Ireland. (City Archives of Antwerp, archives of the Ostend Company, no. 5721; courtesy of Veerle Delahaye and Jan Parmentier.)

Fig. 13 Announcement addressed to potential freighters to load a French frigate set to depart Ostend for several Spanish ports and Marseille (1723). The Patrick Sarsfield referred to in this document was from Cork and had arrived in Ostend in 1716. Thomas Ray took him into his merchant house, and the two entered a seven-year agreement to handle cargoes belonging to East India merchants based in the port. However, their partnership lasted only two years, as Sarsfield preferred to concentrate on large-scale smuggling of East India goods into Ireland and England among other places. Although he made a considerable fortune, Sarsfield's smuggling eventually led to his undoing. (Heemkundige Kring 'De Plate', Oostende, no. 425/97; courtesy of Jan Parmentier.)

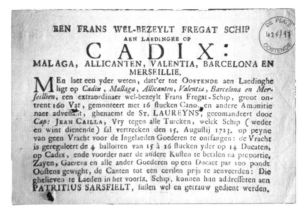

Fig. 14 Bernardo Valois (1663–1727). Born into a Waterford merchant family, Bernardo Valois (Bernard Walsh) left Ireland for Ostend in 1679. Five years later he joined his brother Patrick in Tenerife, where he trained as a merchant. He consolidated his lucrative commercial partnerships with the Fitzgerald family through his marriage to Francisca Xaviera Fitzgerald of Nantes in 1705. Walsh became one of the richest Irish merchants in Tenerife and held the post of consul of the Irish nation in the Canaries. A devout Catholic, he financed the construction of the chapel of St Patrick, or 'The Irish chapel', in the parish church in Puerto de la Cruz, where he and several other Irish are buried. (Courtesy of the Cologan family, Tenerife, Spain; photo © Manuel Días Febles.)

111

Figs 15 and 16 (above and opposite) Gregorio Fitzgerald (eighteenth century), 'Primo y suegro de Bernardo Valois' (cousin and in-law of Bernard Walsh); Nicolás Bernardo Valois Geraldin (1706–41), son of Bernardo Valois. The Fitzgeralds (Geraldins) and Walshes (Valois), both originally from Waterford, ranked among the most successful Irish financiers and merchants in eighteenth-century western Europe, with close connections between their major family branches in London, Ostend, Saint-Malo, Nantes and the Canary Islands. In the early 1700s the new attraction of thriving commerce with the Indies,

centred on Cádiz, drew many Irish to settle not only in Spanish coastal ports but also in the Canary Islands, which were a very important outpost for ships using the trade winds for crossing the Atlantic. By the early eighteenth century, the Walshes and Cologans had acquired sizeable fortunes, which enabled them to invest heavily in townhouses, farms, mills, grain stores, shops and wine cellars. (Courtesy of the Cologan family, Tenerife, Spain; photo © Manuel Días Febles.)

114

Fig. 17 Juan Cólogan Blanco (1710–71) and his wife Margarita, née Valois Geraldín (1720–49). A native of Dublin, Juan Cólogan (John Cologan) was head of the biggest merchant house in the Canaries during the eighteenth century. Its success was heavily dependent on close business and familial ties with the thriving port of Cádiz. His marriage to Margarita, daughter of Bernardo Valois, consolidated ties between Tenerife's two leading Irish merchant houses. (Courtesy of the Cologan family, Tenerife, Spain; photo © Manuel Días Febles.)

Fig. 18 Pedro Alonso O'Crouley (1740–1817), c. 1774. In many respects, this highly successful Cádiz-based merchant epitomised the spirit of the Enlightenment in his lifelong enthusiasm for the latest innovations in the arts, sciences, agriculture and commerce and for the antiquities. This was reflected in his membership of several prestigious societies, notably the Real Sociedad Vascongada, which by 1776 boasted a thousand members in Spain, England and America, the Real Sociedad Económica Matritense, which specialised in the study of industrial innovations, and the Society of Antiquaries of Edinburgh. (Museo Histórico Municipal, Cádiz.)

7// Español, y Albino. Tornatras.

8// Español, y Jornatras, tente en el aire.

Figs 19–25 During his sojourn as a youth in Mexico, O'Crouley exhibited a precocious interest in the exotic and alien world around him. His exceptional skill in observing and recording the features of the people, along with the flora and fauna, can be seen from these detailed and colourful illustrations featured in his *Description*. (Biblioteca Nacional de España, Madrid.)

Fig. 19 (opposite) Español, y Albino, Tornatras.

Fig. 20 (opposite) Español , y Fornatras, tente en el aire.

Fig. 21 Yndio, y Chino, Albarazado.

Fig. 22 Yndio, y Negro, Sambaigo.

9 Yndio, y Chino, Albarazado.

10 Yndio, y Negro, Sambaigo.

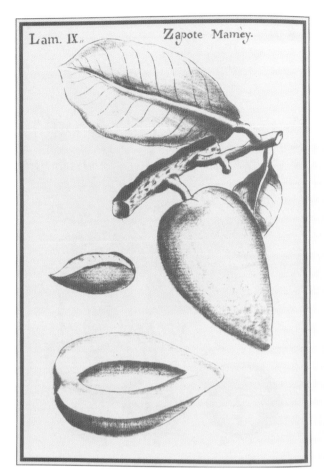

Fig. 23 Zapote Mamèy (Lam. IX).

118

Fig. 24 Granadilla de China (Lam. X).

Fig. 25 Birds of New Spain.

Fig. 26 Saint-Malo in the eighteenth century, from *Histoire de la Revolution Française* by Louis Blanc (1811–82) (engraving), French School (nineteenth century). Saint-Malo was a familiar port of call for Irish merchants and seafarers from the late fifteenth century. It had a reputation as a safe haven for those seeking political and religious asylum from Ireland during the 1500s. From the mid-sixteenth century, a coterie of Irish families including Martins, Kirwans and Lynches settled in this port and maintained strong trade links with Ireland. (© Private collection/Ken Welsh/The Bridgeman Art Library.)

Fig. 28 Charles Edward Stuart (Bonnie Prince Charlie) with Antoine Walsh, before the Battle of Culloden (1746). Antoine Vincent Walsh (1703–63) was one of the Young Stuart Pretender's most loyal and influential supporters in France. He played a prominent role in the Irish émigré community's planning and financing of Stuart's expedition to Scotland, which precipitated the 1745 rising. Charles Edward was conveyed to Scotland on board a ship owned by Walsh, who accompanied him. On his return to France, Walsh unsuccessfully lobbied Louis XV to send aid to the floundering Stuart Pretender, who ultimately suffered a resounding defeat at Culloden. Even after all hope of Charles Edward's cause had faded, Walsh remained a trusted friend for the remainder of his life. (Château de Serrant, 49170 Saint-Georges-sur-Loire, France.)

Fig. 27 View of Saint-Malo (engraving) (b/w photo) by Nicolas Marie Ozanne (1728–1811) (after). By the late 1680s Saint-Malo was home to a small but influential community of Irish merchants and privateers, the most important being the Walsh, Geraldine (Fitzgerald), Kirwan, Porter, White and Brown families. Their close family connections underpinned a trade network that linked Saint-Malo, Nantes and Bordeaux with ports in Ireland and French overseas colonies. Families operating from Ireland facilitated quadrangular trade in which salted Irish beef, butter, herring and lard were sold in Brittany and in the Antilles. In the late seventeenth and the eighteenth century the Irish in Saint-Malo, and specifically the Walshes and Geraldines, were heavily involved in privateering, for which the port became infamous.
(© Bibliothèque nationale, Paris, France/Archives Charmet/The Bridgeman Art Library.)

121

Fig. 29 View of Bordeaux port from Château Trompette, 1759, by Joseph Vernet (1714–1789). (Peinture, inv. no. 5 OA 10 D, © Musée national de la Marine, Paris/L.-S. Jaulmes.)

Fig. 30 Bordeaux in 1776, engraving by Le Gouaz, after Ozanne. In 1776 Richard Hennessy arrived in Bordeaux to start his distilling business, which would have been situated in the Chartrons district (in the background of this engraving), the principal business centre of the port. However, in the early 1780s storm clouds began to gather over the Irish colony in Bordeaux. Although the port maintained a lively connection with Ireland through the brandy trade, for the first time in a century new Irish houses were outnumbered by English firms. Wine consumption in Ireland was beginning to decline. Moreover, Bordeaux's increased trade with England during the 1780s, which was largely handled by the port's Irish firms, gave rise to complacency and a failure to recognise the onset of Bordeaux's decline as one of the world's great ports. (© Musée National de la Marine.)

Fig. 31 Signature of Richard Hennessy (d. 1800), brandy distiller. A native of Ballymacroy, near Mallow in County Cork, Hennessy joined the French army in 1748. His army record describes him as six feet tall with auburn hair, blue eyes and a handsome, freckled, oval face. He was said to have been warm-hearted, kind and convivial company. After a brief military career, he went into the brandy export business, first in Ostend and later in Cognac and Bordeaux. (Courtesy of the Collection Historique Hennessy.)

Fig. 32 The Kirwan family château, the Médoc, Bordeaux region. Built for Sir John Collingwood, an English wine merchant, in the mid-eighteenth century and originally called Château Lasalle, this residence and its vineyards were inherited and renamed in 1781 by Collingwood's son-in-law, Mark Kirwan, a native of Galway. Despite the interruption of the French Revolution, the Kirwans restored the château and improved the quality of the wines before selling the estate in 1858 to a Bordeaux resident. (Photo: Courtesy of Collection Historique Hennessy.)

5. Irish professionals and European reform

The majority of Irish migrants to Europe in the seventeenth and eighteenth centuries joined existing Irish merchant colonies, regiments and colleges. These communities tended to be unstable, acting as halfway houses between Ireland and eventual integration in the host society. Of course, a great number in these communities either could not or did not intend to stay abroad permanently. They returned home after a spell in college or in the army, although some, especially those in business, moved back and forth regularly between Ireland and the Continent. The latter lived, in fact, between several jurisdictions, usually for economic motives. For those whose stay on the Continent was long-term or permanent, some form of integration was almost inevitable. Most of those who integrated fully, by marriage, obtaining citizenship or sheer success, tended to lose touch both with Ireland and with Irish migrant communities.

A very small number of the integrating Irish made their mark on the Continent not as merchants, soldiers or clerics but in the professions, especially banking, medicine, the state service, the arts and literature. An interesting feature of the phenomenon was the extent to which, integration notwithstanding, foreign and even Irish identity was a factor in the individual's professional ascension and achievement.

The key to professional service abroad was access to the higher echelons of the host society. For the great majority of Irish migrants this was not possible. The vagrants who arrived in Spain and France in the early seventeenth century clung precariously to the lower rungs of the social ladders in La Coruña and Paris, just like the demobilised Irish soldiers and their families in France after the French army reforms of 1697. However, for a select minority, access was possible. Catholic clergy, for instance, enjoyed access to French, Spanish, Austrian Imperial and papal social networks, thanks to religious solidarity. From at least the 1580s the Irish presented themselves as victims of religious persecution and called on their Catholic counterparts on the Continent for aid. For clergy this boiled down to educational facilities, financial support and, more rarely, posts, usually unimportant ones, in foreign dioceses. For Catholic nobility like Hugh O'Neill and the O'Sullivan Beare, who had been allies of the Spanish in the early seventeenth-century wars against Elizabeth I, access to social networks took the form of material support, usually renewable money grants, membership of prestigious military orders and vague promises of military assistance in the event of a foreign descent on Ireland to achieve a regime change. Nobly born Irish bolstered their claims on the Spanish, in particular, by regular recourse to the principle of religious solidarity, natural justice and reference to the origins myth that gave the Gaelic Irish nobility and their Spanish counterparts a common Milesian ancestor. In the early seventeenth century the Spanish appointed a special minister for the incoming Irish, who was assisted by the Franciscan Florence Conry in the task of separating the worthy from the less worthy among the waves of incoming Irish migrants. From the Spanish point of view it was important to keep numbers down, to avoid placing extra strain on already taut public finances. Also, the Spanish administration had to reckon with the innate social conservatism of the Spanish elite, which was hostile to foreign elements corrupting its alleged purity of blood. In particular, the Irish, who lived under a Protestant regime at home, were often suspected of heresy and hence held at arm's length by the proudly orthodox Spaniards.

While social access at a high level in a host society was for the very few clergy and nobility who already enjoyed status at home, even for them it was not plain sailing. Although Madrid was ready to support the O'Neills financially, they were consistently refused access to Spain for political reasons. The O'Sullivan Beares managed to gain admission to Spain, but in the second and third generations the family struggled to capitalise on its initial advantages and faded away. Spanish, French and Austrian Imperial societies were governed by strict codes based on blood and religious affiliation. Although the Irish could generally play the religious card, it was more difficult to prove noble birth, especially given the extremely lax record-keeping characteristic of early modern Irish society. When it proved impossible to provide documentary proof of noble birth, high-born Irish migrants relied on the testimonies of clergy, family and foreign patrons. This meant that Irish access to the upper echelons of foreign societies remained limited throughout the seventeenth century.

It was not until the late seventeenth and the early eighteenth century that the migrating Irish began to enjoy strategic social access to European societies. The regime change effected in Ireland by the deposition of James II, his military defeat and his subsequent exile in France obliged Louis XIV, James's ally, to make provision not only for James but also for his dependants, many of them Irish of high birth. When the Treaty of Limerick permitted thousands of Irish soldiers in James's service to follow him to France, Louis XIV accepted them into his military machine, eventually as Irish regiments under French command.

The Jacobite migration was not only military in character. Officers and soldiers were accompanied by their families and a network of professionals and officials, who ensured that the patrimony of the exiled Jacobites was appropriately managed. Typical of this breed of Jacobite was the Irish merchant Daniel Arthur (1625?–1705). He had operated originally in Ireland and later, in the 1660s, in London but had been forced to leave England owing to anti-Catholic hysteria in the 1670s. He moved to France, settling in Paris, where he established a banking concern. His activities received a major boost with the arrival of the Jacobites in the 1690s. Arthur assumed responsibility for the management of their financial affairs and was assisted by other Irish bankers. He was notably associated with Richard Cantillon, a relation of the economist of the same name. Arthur played a crucial role in facilitating the circulation of funds and capital among the exiled Irish and English Jacobites. He developed a broad network of clients not only in Paris but also in the French ports, especially among Irish merchants settled in Dunkirk, Saint-Malo, Brest and Nantes. He was careful to maintain his links with Ireland and continued to employ people from his own part of the country in his French offices. In his will he left the considerable sum of nearly 100,000 livres; his extensive clientele was inherited eventually by Richard Cantillon. In the next generation, Irish bankers like John Waters were successful in Paris. His father George had left Ireland with the Jacobites in 1691 and had set up a bank in Paris. John succeeded his father in 1752. He developed a good relationship with the Irish college in Paris. Arthur and Waters were useful not only to displaced Jacobites but also to the French, who welcomed the arrival of business talent to their economy. An important body of French public opinion was anxious to reform state finances according to English models. Arthur, Waters and others served as conduits into France for modernising business methods.

Others in the Jacobite entourage gained access to privileged positions abroad thanks to a combination of natural talent, strategic knowledge and usefulness to the host administration. Nathaniel Hooke (1664–1738) began his career as a religious radical in the Dutch provinces, where he supported the Monmouth Rebellion against James II in 1685. He subsequently converted to Catholicism, supported James II, was present at the Battle of the Boyne in 1690 and later entered service in the Irish regiment of Galmoy in France. After his discharge in 1697, Hooke, like so many other Irish soldiers, was without resources. He was still associated with the Jacobites, taking part in missions to Scotland in 1705 and 1707; however, he was obliged to seek professional advancement elsewhere. His erstwhile alliance with Protestant radicals and his intimate knowledge of both England and the Dutch provinces made him a valuable espionage and diplomatic resource to the government of Louis XIV. Hooke used his experience as a spy and diplomat in the Dutch provinces on the eve of the Wars of the Spanish Succession. He later saw service, for France, in Saxony but was also considered as Jacobite representative in Vienna and later, in 1718, was appointed James III's representative in Berlin.

The French were happy to avail of Hooke's services and of the banking experience of Irish migrants like Arthur and Waters, who knew the English and Irish money systems. In general, Irish migrants who brought particular skills were welcomed in host jurisdictions and were often given preferential treatment, usually in the form of social status, access to economic networks and occasionally grants of land and titles. A similar phenomenon was discernible in Sweden. According to state law there, Catholics were prohibited from engaging in a broad range of activities, but, when Irish entrepreneurs like Denis O'Brien and John O'Kelly arrived in eighteenth-century Stockholm with industrial expertise potentially valuable to the Swedish economy, an exception was made and access was allowed. In Spain, where the activities of English and Scots Protestant merchants were limited by law, Irish merchants sometimes acted as fronts for barred British companies and interests. This made the Irish merchant colonies in the Spanish ports and islands valuable to Spanish entrepreneurs desirous of circumventing the restrictive legislation.

The density and relative success of Irish migrants in eighteenth-century Paris permitted the formation of an Irish Freemasons' lodge in the city. The l'Irlandaise du Soleil Levant lodge was composed mainly of doctors, medical students and not a few priests. Paris, like Montpellier and Rheims, was a popular training place for medical students, many of whom frequented the Irish ecclesiastical colleges in the city before opting for their chosen profession. Timothy O'Scanlan, from Newcastle in County Limerick, studied in Paris from 1748 to 1756. There, he qualified as a medical doctor before moving to Spain, where he acted as medical officer of one of the Irish regiments. In Spain he pioneered the practice of smallpox inoculation, publishing three works on the subject, one at the request of the Royal Academy of Medicine in Madrid. He was at one time chief consultant physician to the Spanish armies. He also distinguished himself in his care of French soldiers fighting in Spain. Another Irishman,

Daniel O'Sullivan (b. 1760) from Kilcoe in County Cork, completed his initial medical studies in Toulouse and Montpellier before eventually setting sail from Cádiz for Veracruz as surgeon to the second battalion of the Puebla infantry regiment. Once in Mexico, O'Sullivan became head surgeon in the syphilis department of the hospital of San Andrés, Mexico City.

The French–Spanish corridor opened by the arrival of a branch of the French Bourbons to the Spanish throne in the early eighteenth century was familiar to many Irish migrants. It provided, in particular, entry to Spain for Irish military personnel, who joined the Bourbon administration in Madrid in a number of capacities. Under Ferdinando VI the Spanish Bourbons favoured reformist policies, generally aimed at modernising the army, the economy and the administration, along the lines of northern European states. A number of Irish were available to provide the expertise needed. The most extraordinary of these was Ricardo Wall (1694–1777), whose family origins were in Limerick. His family had been part of the Jacobite migration to France, and he subsequently moved to Spain, seeing service there from 1718. He later served in Italy and the West Indies. In 1747 he was in the Spanish delegation at the negotiations for the Treaty of Aix-la-Chapelle (1748), and he was appointed to the Spanish embassy in London later that year. His main concern as ambassador was to negotiate favourable commercial arrangements for Spain and to bring northern technical progress south, especially in shipbuilding and the wool industry. Wall was a loyal servant of the Spanish Bourbons and worked with the Spanish secretary of state, Carvajal, to protect Spanish interests in trade and diplomacy. On Carvajal's death Wall reluctantly returned to Spain, where he acted as foreign minister and later as secretary of state, or prime minister. Although his administration was compromised by internal conflicts revolving around centralising policies, such as the campaign against the Jesuits, and the aristocratic conservatism of Spanish courtiers, Wall made a considerable contribution to the development of

Spanish public policy. After the death of Ferdinando VI in 1759 and the accession of Carlos III, he was less in favour but was frequently consulted on state business. In retirement he paid great attention to his estates and to the economic condition of his tenants. His entourage included military men and administrators of the calibre of Alexander O'Reilly (d. 1794) and counted economists like Bernard Ward, who made an important contribution to the Spanish debate on economic modernisation.

In Austria a similar pattern emerged. From the early seventeenth century, Irishmen there had opportunistically acted as colonel-proprietors offering to raise regiments for the decentralised Austrian service. Estimates vary, but perhaps a total of 1500 Irish or Austrian-born Irish served over the period. They were a compact group that benefited from the goodwill and contacts created by their initial activities in the Imperial service. Their social origin in Ireland was narrow, and by the eighteenth century they were no longer recruiting any rank and file in Ireland. They were increasingly of Austrian birth and developed in the eighteenth century as a sort of power elite, which was well represented in Austrian military councils and in the Imperial foreign service. They were also prominent in the political administration of the Austrian Lowlands and, almost uniquely among the Irish power elites of the *Ancien Régime*, survived and even prospered in the nineteenth century. Field Marshal Francis Maurice Lacy (1725–1801) was typical of second-generation Irish migrants who attained high administrative office in the Austrian Imperial armies. Born in St Petersburg, he served in the War of the Austrian Succession in the 1740s. After a distinguished active career he oversaw major reforms in the Austrian Imperial military establishment, enjoying the favour of both Empress Maria Theresa and her son, Joseph II.

Interwoven with the network of Irish migrant professionals was a looser association of intellectuals, artists and writers, many on the move for personal reasons or simply to experience the variety and stimulus of the Continent. A great number of these were associated with Catholic intellectual circles. Irish thinkers like the Leuven-, Rome- and Prague-based Franciscans John Sinnich, Michael Moore and Luke Joseph Hooke gained access to European academic networks and made valuable contributions to contemporary debates in their fields, establishing something of a displaced Irish Catholic intelligentsia in Europe. They provided an essential conduit between Ireland and the Continent, with intellectual traffic moving in both directions. The mid-seventeenth century was an especially significant period of intellectual exchange. If Séathrún Céitinn and Mícheál Ó Cléirigh, two of the century's leading Irish historians, did not know the work of the Spanish theologian and political thinker Francisco Suárez, their portrayal of the Irish community as one rooted in a common language and customary laws was compatible with the Spanish philosopher's notion of the *ius gentium*, or universal rights of people. Philip O'Sullivan Beare elaborated the theoretical significance of this Irish tradition of customary law in terms of an international theory of natural law. His treatment of natural law as a means of influencing Spain to side with the cause of justice of the kingdom of Ireland was a significant attempt to rationalise and justify Irish efforts to lure the Spaniards back to military intervention in Ireland.

For these intellectuals the experience of exile was far from negative. Displacement opened fresh opportunities to Irish Catholic thought and introduced scholars, pastors and ecclesiastics to new intellectual trends, providing them with access to a wider European audience. It was also hugely important for artists, especially in the visual and plastic arts in the eighteenth century. Nicholas Blakey (*fl.* 1747–78) and John Forster (*fl.* 1773–80) lived and studied in Paris; Christopher Hewetson (*fl.* 1772–94) studied in Rome; and Nathaniel Hone (1718–84) travelled between Rome and Florence. James Barry (1741–1806) also worked in Italy. Further north, James Latham (1696–47) studied in Antwerp, and Frederick O'Ferral was mint-master at Dresden. Like

Irish artists, migrant Irish thinkers engaged with the fundamental intellectual and political developments of their time: the question of national identity, the rise of mechanistic science, the secularisation of politics, the challenges of religious innovation and the Enlightenment. In the context of religious innovation and intellectual change, the career of the Donegal-born John Toland (1670–1722) is especially significant, indicating that the Irish migrant move to the Continent was by no means exclusively either Jacobite or Catholic. Toland was the author of the controversial critique of traditional religion *Christianity not mysterious* (1696). He was also an inveterate traveller and typical of a generation of Irish intellectuals who were as at home in Paris or Berlin as in Dublin or Cork. Born into a Catholic, Gaelic-speaking family, he converted to Anglicanism and thereby gained access to patronage networks otherwise closed to him. A student in Glasgow, he was part of the English embassy in Hanover in 1701 and was in Berlin the following year, where he was in contact with Leibniz. He then travelled to Holland, where he met Pierre Bayle and contributed a materialistic account of the soul for his famous *Dictionary*. He subsequently returned to England, where he attacked Newtonian physics and won a reputation as a critic of external explanation for internal events. This consecrated him as a critic of traditional Tory politics, which so revered inherited institutions like monarchy and state church. In 1707 Toland was again on the Continent, this time in Düsseldorf, Hanover, Berlin and Vienna. He also spent time in Prague, where he visited the local community of Irish Franciscans. Despite religious and ideological differences, the friars were happy to provide their countryman with a testimonial. Toland commented:

Yet I did not receive half that satisfaction from their many civilities to my own person, as I was charm'd with their putting round the Queen's health [Queen Anne] in full refectory, where a great many strangers were present, and of several nations as well as of different Religions. Nor did I find 'em less easy and well-bred upon this last article than in other things; tho' I frankly told 'em my sentiment and perhaps that I might, sometimes, to improve by the discourse of ingenious persons carry matter further than Reason or the Reformation will allow.

He stayed on in Holland, where he researched ancient Christianity, especially the Celtic variety, and advocated the granting of civil rights to Jews. In 1711 he returned to England, where he developed his reputation as a proponent of pantheism. Toland was a permanent affront to what passed for propriety in his time, and his career demonstrates the importance of intellectual exchange for the evolution of political thought, scientific enquiry and critical analysis.

Although Toland's questioning of accepted religious beliefs and their associated texts was not typical of the Irish intellectual diaspora in the *Ancien Régime*, it underlines the disruptive potential of intellectual exchange for political, religious and cultural establishments in both the sending and the host society. The migrant Irish, though largely associated with established state and ecclesiastical elites in Europe, had the potential, owing to their political and religious exclusion in Ireland, to develop harsh critiques of what they regarded as the exercise of arbitrary power. Some were attracted to the radical and republican political ideas that became more popular in Europe on the eve of the French Revolution, Wolfe Tone being just one example. Paradoxically, it was precisely this sort of critique of the old European order that opened the way to its demise in the political, social and economic changes heralded by the French Revolution. The fall of the old order signalled the end of the European system that had provided professional and intellectual niches for Irish migrants like Arthur, Wall and Toland.

Fig. 1 Arthur Richard Dillon, archbishop of Narbonne (1721–1806). Born at Saint-Germain-en-Laye, Paris, the fifth son of Arthur Dillon, head of the Dillon regiment in the French service, Arthur Richard was appointed archbishop of Narbonne in 1763. An eloquent orator and capable administrator, Dillon was exceptional among Irishmen in attaining high political office, serving as president of both the États of Languedoc and the assembly of French clergy. He was a great builder and was responsible for the construction of the junction between the Narbonne inland waterway and the famous 'canal du Midi'. This piece of infrastructure enabled Narbonne to reintegrate the transport networks of the south of France and was a major boost to the local economy. Richard was a great intellectual patron, in the best Enlightenment tradition. Thanks to him, the Académie des Sciences in Montpellier acquired the famous Hôtel de Builleminet, where it installed its library and conservatory of natural history. He founded technical colleges in Toulouse and Montpellier and reopened the archaeological digs in the Roman remains of Nimes. Dillon's opposition to the Civil Constitution of the Clergy in the 1790s earned him the enmity of the French Revolutionaries and resulted in the loss of his archbishopric. He fled to England, where he died. (Courtesy of the Pelican and Coronet Company and the Hon. Isabel Cobbe.)

Fig. 2 A model of the Newcomen Steam Engine. This steam engine, the predecessor to the Watt Engine, was developed during the 1700s. In the 1720s the Irish entrepreneur Colonel John O'Kelly made an unsuccessful attempt to secure a licence to build Sweden's first Newcomen Steam Engine. Despite O'Kelly's being 'en Catholisk Irlädsk adelsman', the Swedes, like confessional authorities elsewhere in Europe, tended to turn a blind eye to religious differences when technology and innovation were in question. The Irish in Europe in the eighteenth century frequently acted as conduits for technology and information transfer between European countries. The complexity of their identity, the flexibility of their political loyalties and their openness to innovation made them popular as agents of modernising European administrations. (Science Museum, London / Science & Society Picture Library.)

Fig. 3 Daniel O'Riordan, an Irish medic in seventeenth-century Toulouse, 1650s. According to available records, nearly 400 Irish students attended the universities of Toulouse and Cahors in France during the seventeenth and eighteenth centuries, the great majority from Munster. Although the Irish college in Toulouse was founded to train priests for the Irish mission, by the eighteenth century the number of Irish university students following theology courses was exceeded by the number of those studying medicine. It was not uncommon for Irish theology students, including some who were eventually ordained priests, to take courses in the faculty of medicine, a practice virtually unheard of among their French counterparts. Daniel O'Riordan, who features in this rare contemporaneous portrait now housed in the School of Pharmacy, Toulouse, was active in Toulouse in the mid-seventeenth century. He was prominent in the university and a respected medic in the Hôtel Dieu. (Université de Toulouse and Patrick Ferté.)

Fig. 4 Ricardo Wall (1694–1777), by an anonymous artist (eighteenth century). Wall was the most successful of all of the Irish migrants to Spain. His loyalty to the Bourbon administration was solid but did not deter him from implementing reforms, which were often unpopular with entrenched and powerful interests. '[I] hold the Spanish monarchy in all the esteem in the world, and I have always been ready to sacrifice my life to pay for the services I have received' (letter from Ricardo Wall to State Minister Carvajal, 4 December 1749). (Museo Naval, Madrid.)

PROYECTO
ECONOMICO,

en que se proponen varias providencias, di-
rigidas á promover los intereses de España,
con los medios y fondos necesarios pa-
ra su plantificacion:

ESCRITO EN EL AñO DE 1762

*Por D. BERNARDO WARD, del Consejo de
S. M. y su Ministro de la Real Junta de
Comercio y Moneda.*

OBRA POSTUMA.

MADRID. MDCCLXXIX.

Por D. JOACHIN IBARRA, Impresor de Cámara de S. M.

Con las licencias necesarias.

Fig. 5 Title page of Bernardo Ward's *Proyecto Economico...* (Madrid, 1779). Of Irish descent, Ward, who was in the employment of King Ferdinando VI of Spain, travelled throughout Europe to study various means of ameliorating the state of the poor and to promote trade and manufacturing in Spain. In 1762 he wrote his considered and detailed report, which also presented his proposal for reform. Regarded as perhaps the best-composed and most methodical work written on political economy in eighteenth-century Spain, Ward's *Proyecto* was published posthumously in 1779 and reprinted twice during the 1780s. (Russell Library, National University of Ireland, Maynooth, from the collections of St Patrick's College, Maynooth.)

136|

Fig. 6 Bust of Luke Joseph Hooke (1714–96), Catholic theologian, professor of ancient languages, librarian. Born in Dublin, Hooke studied theology at the University of Paris and in 1742 was appointed professor of theology there, although he lost his chair owing to faculty politics. He subsequently held the post of professor of Hebrew and Chaldean at the university and was chief librarian at the prestigious Mazarine Library. Among his most influential publications were his *Principia* (1752–4), which sought to build bridges between traditional theology and the new science of the Enlightened era, and his *Principes sur l'origine, la nature, la souveraineté, l'étendue et l'alliance des deux puissances* (1791), which argued strongly for the independence of the church *vis-à-vis* the state in the Revolutionary era. (Bibliothèque Mazarine.)

Fig. 7 Engraving of John Toland, philosopher and freethinker (1670–1722), from U.G. Thorschmid's *Versuch einer Vollstandige Englandische Freydenker Bibilothek…*, vol. 3 (1766). Irish intellectuals contributed to the European world of thought and letters. The Irish Franciscans in Leuven, Rome and Prague were central figures in seventeenth-century Scotism. Irish historians like Thomas Messingham in Paris and David Rothe, who was educated in Douai, applied European standards to the writing of Irish history. Economists like Bernardo Ward made important contributions to public-policy making in Bourbon Spain. The Donegal-born John Toland enjoyed an international reputation as a philosopher and freethinker. He used his frequent and extensive European travels to broaden his intellectual experience. (The Beinecke Rare Book and Manuscript Library.)

Fig. 8 The Taking of the Bastille, 14th July 1789 (oil on canvas), by Jean-Pierre Houel (1735–1813). By the end of the eighteenth century, changes at home and in Europe began to impinge negatively on Irish activities on the Continent. The Irish found military careers on the Continent less attractive because of improved opportunities at home, in the East India Company forces and in the British army. Increasing instability in France put pressure on the Irish there, whom the Revolutionaries considered to be national liabilities because of their foreign status, their noble backgrounds and their Catholicism. When the French Revolution spread into Spain and the Low Countries, migrant Irish communities and institutions felt the pinch. In the nineteenth century the Irish turned toward the Atlantic world and the professional opportunities offered them by the burgeoning British Empire. They remained a force in Europe after the Revolution but not on the scale enjoyed in the eighteenth century. (Musée de la Ville de Paris, Musée Carnavalet, Paris, France/The Bridgeman Art Library.)

6. Pedigrees: social status and integration

The following selection of arms and pedigrees is from the 'Irish Nobility' manuscript armorials and the 'Registered Pedigrees' (the 'Wild Geese Registers') in the Office of the Chief Herald of Ireland, Kildare Street, Dublin. The eighteenth century witnessed a significant increase in the official activities and responsibilities of the Office of Arms. In the wake of James II's deposition in 1689, thousands of Irish Catholics who emigrated to the Continent encountered significant challenges as they endeavoured to gain admission to a rigid aristocratic society in which marriage into the ranks of the local nobility, commissions in the army and admission to court all relied on possession of an attested family tree and an authentic coat of arms. Pedigrees had to be authenticated by the appropriate authority in the home country. The immense importance of the Office of Arms to the Irish émigré population is illustrated by the fact that approximately half of all pedigrees registered in the Office between 1750 and 1800 relate to Irish families living in Europe. Indeed, in the early 1790s, the King of Arms, Sir Chichester Fortescue, proved more than willing to be of assistance to such émigré families. In 1792 he made it known to Monsieur Henri Shee at the Palais Royal in Paris that:

> If any family in France may in the future want the assistance of the Office of Arms to prove their kindred here, it would be well to correspond with the King of Arms…I as King of Arms have great pleasure in answering your letter.

It is significant that the Office was willing to facilitate the integration abroad of these descendants of Jacobite émigrés who, in the 1690s, had been dispossessed of their land and forced into exile by the political regime with which the Office itself was so closely identified.

The Irish Nobility manuscript armorials, from which the Tyrone and Tyrconnell arms are taken, contain emblazoned achievements of members of Ireland's nobility during the reign of Elizabeth I and feature depictions of ancient, medieval and modern dynastic symbols of Ireland.

The Registered Pedigrees series is largely a register of patents and certifications issued by the Office of Arms during the second half of the eighteenth century to Irish noblemen on the Continent, especially Spain, France and Austria.

Hughe o Neyle Erle of Tyrone,

Fig. 1 Earl of Tyrone's arms, Irish Nobility C, from GO MS 32, fol. 6.

142

Fig. 3 De Lacy pedigree, from GO MS 162, fol. 112.

Fig. 2 (opposite) Tyrconnell's arms, Irish Nobility E, from GO MS 34, fol. 12.

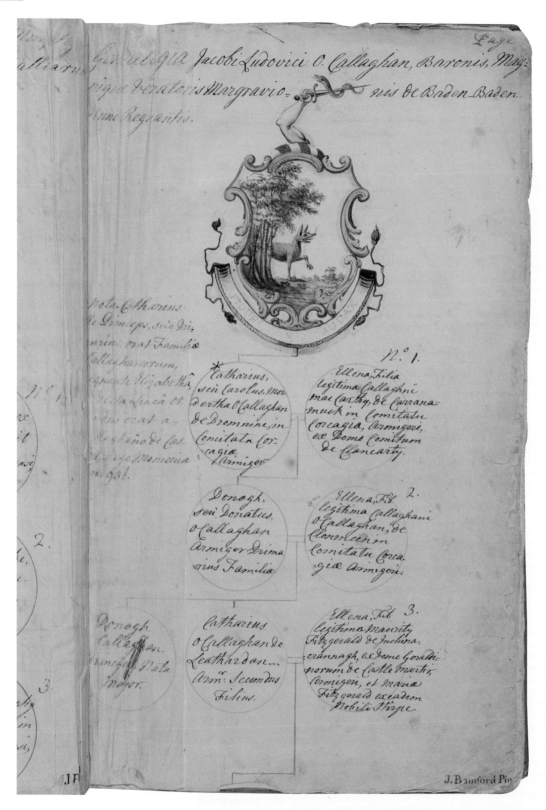

Fig. 4 O'Callaghan pedigree, from GO MS 165, fol. 3.

145

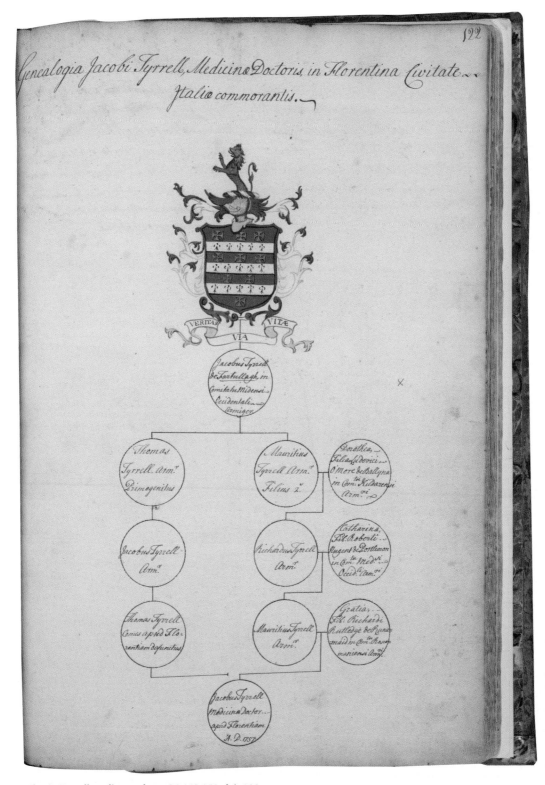

Fig. 5 Tyrrell pedigree, from GO MS 162, fol. 122.

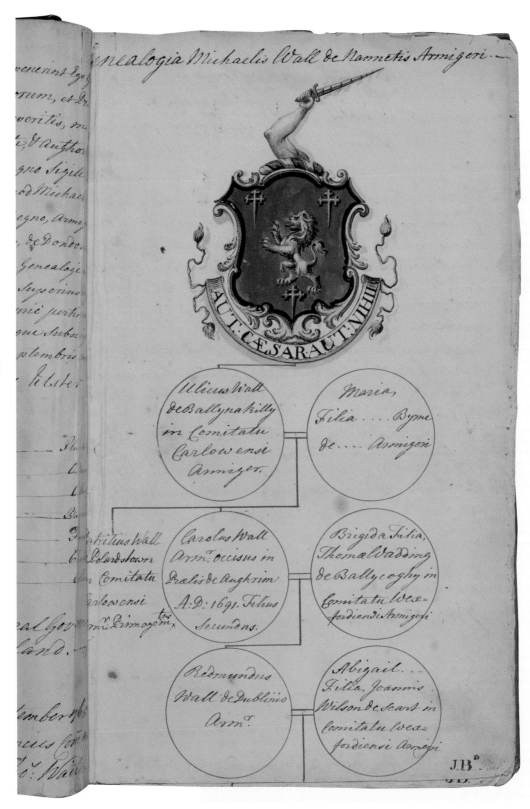

Fig. 6 Wall pedigree, from GO MS 165, fol. 78.

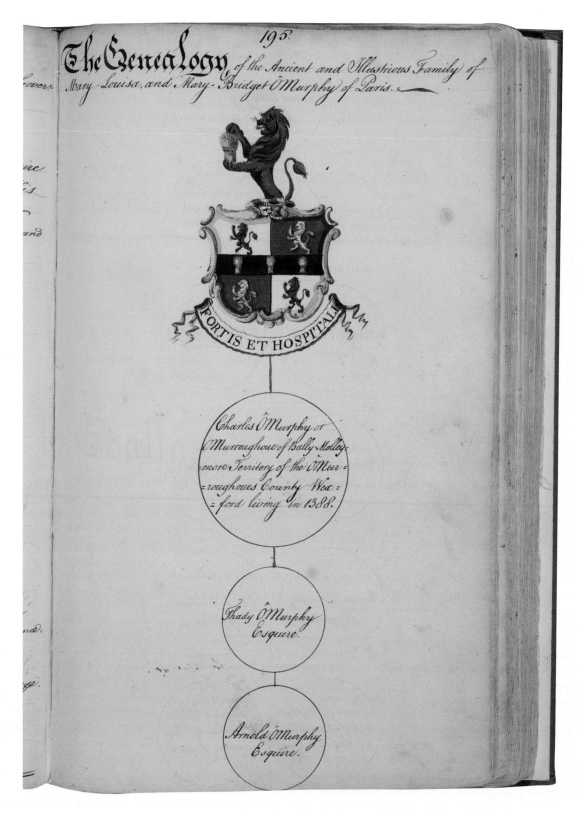

195.

The Genealogy *of the Ancient and Illustrious Family of Mary-Louisa, and Mary-Bridget O'Murphy of Paris.*

FORTIS ET HOSPITALI

Charles O'Murphy or O'Murroughoue of Bally-Molley-more Territory of the O'Mur-roughoues County Wex-ford living in 1388.

Thady O'Murphy Esquire.

Arnold O'Murphy Esquire.

Fig. 7 (a) O'Murphy pedigree, from GO MS 165, fol. 195.

**Fig 7 (b) Girl Resting/Ruhendes Mädchen
(Miss O'Murphy)** (oil on canvas) by François
Boucher (1752). Marie-Louise O'Murphy
(1737–1814), was the daughter of an Irish solider
turned cobbler in Rouen. On his death, Marie-
Louise's mother took her to Paris, where the young
girl got work as a model and famously posed for
Louis XV's official painter, François Boucher in
1752. The resulting painting of *Girl on a Couch*
was more racily called *The Sprawling Miss Murphy*
and caused a scandal. Louis was unabashed and
had taken Miss 'Morfi' as one of his mistresses. A
contemporaneous pamphlet criticising Louis'
general sexual predation had him defend his
conduct by saying 'it is necessary for my people to
make sacrifices for me'. Marie-Louise had at least
one daughter by him but was soon supplanted by
the king's main mistress, Madame de Pompadour.
An arranged marriage and exile followed. Miss
'Morfi' continued to act as a courtesan but never
regained the king's exclusive favour. She survived
the Revolution, living on to witness the fall of
Napoleon. (Bayerische Staatsgemäldesammlungen,
Alte Pinakothek Munich, inv. no. 1166.)

Fig. 9 King Louis XV of France (1710–74), studio of Louis-Michel van Loo. (© By kind permission of the Trustees of the Wallace Collection, London (P477).)

Fig. 8 (left) La marquise de Pompadour (1721–64) by Maurice Quentin de La Tour (1704–88). (Photo: RMN; © Gérard Blot.)

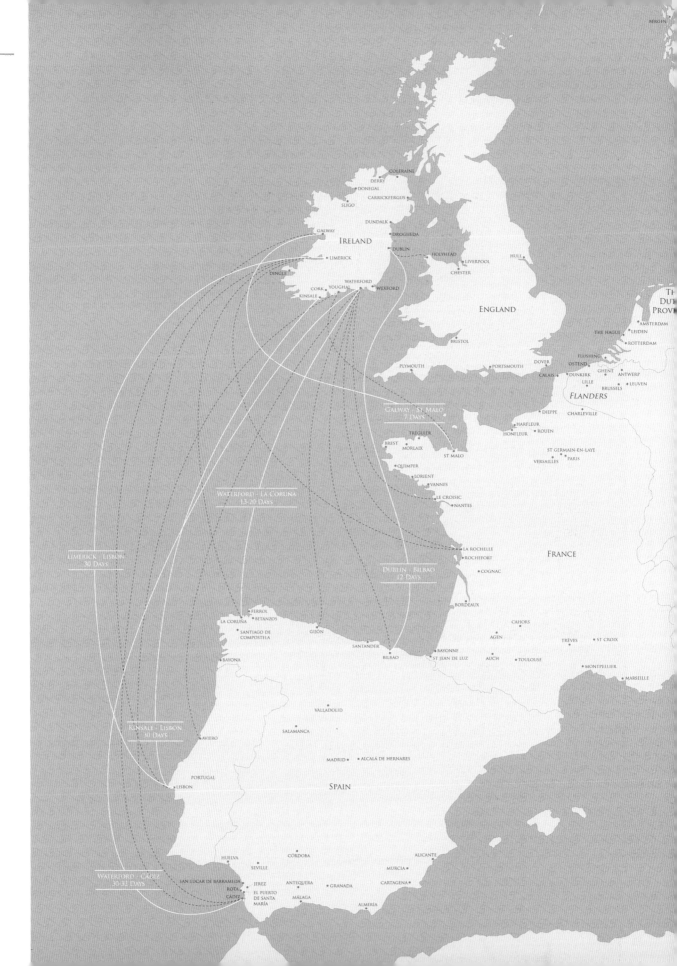

BERGEN

COLERAINE
DERRY
DONEGAL
CARRICKFERGUS
SLIGO
DUNDALK
GALWAY
DROGHEDA
IRELAND
DUBLIN
LIMERICK
HOLYHEAD
LIVERPOOL
HULL
CHESTER
DINGLE
WATERFORD
CORK
YOUGHAL
WEXFORD
KINSALE

ENGLAND

BRISTOL

PLYMOUTH
PORTSMOUTH
DOVER
CALAIS

THE
DUT
PROV

AMSTERDAM
THE HAGUE
LEIDEN
ROTTERDAM
FLUSHING
OSTEND
GHENT
ANTWERP
DUNKIRK
LILLE
LEUVEN
BRUSSELS
FLANDERS

DIEPPE
CHARLEVILLE

GALWAY - ST MALO
7 DAYS

HARFLEUR
TRÉGUIER
HONFLEUR
ROUEN
BREST
MORLAIX
ST GERMAIN-EN-LAYE
ST MALO
VERSAILLES
PARIS
QUIMPER
LORIENT
VANNES
WATERFORD - LA CORUÑA
13-20 DAYS
LE CROISIC
NANTES

LA ROCHELLE
ROCHEFORT
FRANCE
LIMERICK - LISBON
30 DAYS
DUBLIN - BILBAO
12 DAYS
COGNAC

BORDEAUX

CAHORS
FERROL
LA CORUÑA
BETANZOS
AGEN
TRÈVES
ST CROIX
SANTIAGO DE
COMPOSTELA
GIJÓN
SANTANDER
BAYONNE
AUCH
TOULOUSE
BAYONA
BILBAO
ST JEAN DE LUZ
MONTPELLIER
MARSEILLE

VALLADOLID

KINSALE - LISBON
30 DAYS
SALAMANCA
AVIERO

MADRID
ALCALÁ DE HERNARES

PORTUGAL
SPAIN
LISBON

HUELVA
CÓRDOBA
ALICANTE
SEVILLE
MURCIA
WATERFORD - CÁDIZ
30-32 DAYS
SAN LÚCAR DE BARRAMEDA
JEREZ
ANTEQUERA
GRANADA
CARTAGENA
ROTA
EL PUERTO
DE SANTA
MARÍA
CÁDIZ
MÁLAGA
ALMERÍA

Fig. 9 Map showing Irish settlements in Early Modern Europe and travel times.
People, ideas and goods have always moved over and back between Ireland and Europe. This human traffic, over land and by sea, took well-established trade routes to the Continent. In tiny craft, unemployed military and dispossessed aristocracy jostled for space with itinerant academics, dislocated clergy and droves of vagrants. Armed with little more than their wits and often at odds with one another, these political, religious and economic migrants faced an uncertain future abroad. European authorities felt duty bound to cater for aristocracy and military; religious sentiment ensured that clergy were generally well received. Vagrants and beggars, however, met with a cold reception. Over time migrants formed communities and eventually integrated into their host societies. (Courtesy of Martello Media.)

6. Conclusion: new horizons

How many Irish people migrated to continental Europe in the seventeenth and eighteenth centuries? How many returned home? How did their departure affect Ireland and their receiving societies? How did their relationship with Ireland and with the Irish at home evolve? How did the slowdown in migration to Europe from the mid-eighteenth century onwards and the resultant weakening of familial and intellectual ties with the Continent impact Irish society in the nineteenth century? Why had the Irish presence in Europe waned several decades before the French Revolution?

These are some of the most challenging questions facing Irish and European scholars who study Irish migration to continental Europe in the early modern period. Exciting new developments are afoot in this thriving field of research. In archives from Sweden and Spain to the Caribbean and Mexico City, researchers are uncovering the trail of Irish émigrés and reconstructing their unique and fascinating life stories. Indeed, the continuing discovery of the great extent of Irish people's involvement in French, Spanish and Dutch overseas colonial administrations and military orders is a particularly engaging aspect of recent research into the Irish abroad.

Although it is impossible to calculate the total number of Irish who left for the Continent in this period, researchers who have painstakingly sifted through army and university records have been amply rewarded for their efforts through the discovery of significant numbers of Irish. We now know, for example, that there were in excess of 16,000 Irish rank-and-file soldiers serving in France, the vast majority from the 1690s onwards. There were also well over 1,000 Irish clerical students registered at the University of Leuven between *c.* 1550 and the French Revolution; more than 1,500 attended the universities of Paris and Toulouse during the same period. A cursory glance through the records of the faculty of medicine in the University of Rheims in north-eastern France reveals that over 400 Irish students gained degrees in this institution from the 1610s up to the Revolution. Furthermore, as researchers continue to broaden their study of Irish migrants to include the marginalised and vulnerable groups, records are coming to light of an Irish presence in unexpected places. A trawl through the archives of hospitals such as La Charité in Paris has yielded vignettes of the lives and deaths of over 400 Irish men, women and children who were treated there from the early 1690s to 1730. Testimony to the failure of many Irish to adapt effectively to life abroad appears in the sprinkling of 167 Irishmen's names among those who were sent to the French galleys between the 1690s and the 1710s.

While progress in enumerating this migrant population remains steady but slow, two exciting developments in the field have greatly accelerated the process. Firstly, collaboration between scholars in the field has been greatly enhanced by the research network established and maintained by the Irish in Europe Project (www.irishineurope.com) and associated research centres in Ireland and abroad. Secondly, the Irish in Europe Project is developing an electronic research platform to facilitate shared access to the rapidly expanding store of archival data on the Irish. The platform is already beginning to provide researchers with the information technology infrastructure needed to support collaborative research in the field. This twenty-first-century fusion of information technology and historical research is utterly transforming scholarship in the area, opening previously unimagined possibilities for studying the constantly shifting dynamics that characterised the varied and intriguing experience of the Irish in Europe and beyond in the early modern era.

Further reading

Bilbao Acedos, A., *The Irish community in the Basque Country, 1700–1800* (Dublin, 2003).

Canny, Nicholas (ed.), *Europeans on the move: studies on European migration, 1500–1800* (Oxford, 1994).

Chambers, Liam, *Michael Moore, c. 1639–1726: provost of Trinity, rector of Paris* (Irish in Europe Monographs) (Dublin, 2005).

Clarke de Dromantin, Patrick, *Les réfugiés jacobites dans la France du XVIIIe siècle* (Bordeaux, 2005).

Corp, Edward (ed.), *L'autre exil: les Jacobites en France au début du XVIIIe siècle* (Paris and Montpellier, 1993).

Cullen, L.M., *The Irish brandy houses of eighteenth-century France* (Dublin, 2000).

Dagier, P., *Les réfugiés irlandais au 17ème siècle en Finistère* (Quimper, 1999).

Dickson, David, Parmentier, Jan and Ohlmeyer, J.H. (eds), *Irish and Scottish mercantile networks in Europe and overseas in the seventeenth and eighteenth centuries* (Ghent, 2007).

García Hernán, Enrique, *Irlanda y el rey prudente* (2 vols, Madrid, 1999–2003).

García Hernán, Enrique and Recio Morales, Óscar (eds), *Extranjeros en el ejército* (Madrid, 2007).

García Hernán, Enrique *et al.* (eds), *Irlanda y la monarquía Hispánica: Kinsale 1601–2001: guerra, política, exilio y religión* (Madrid, 2002).

Gargett, G. and Sheridan, G. (eds), *Ireland and the French Enlightenment, 1700–1800* (Dublin, 1999).

Genet-Rouffiac, Nathalie, *Le grand exil* (Paris, 2007).

Gillespie, Raymond, *Seventeenth-century Ireland: making Ireland modern* (Dublin, 2006).

Gillespie, Raymond and Hadfield, Andrew (eds), *The Oxford history of the Irish book. III. The Irish book in English, 1550–1800* (Oxford, 2006).

Guimerá Ravina, Agustín, *Burguesía extranjera y comercio atlántico; la empresa comercial irlandesa en Canarias, 1703–1771* (Santa Cruz de Tenerife, 1985).

Henry, Gráinne, *The Irish military community in Spanish Flanders, 1586–1621* (Dublin, 1992).

Kerney Walsh, Micheline, *'Destruction by peace': Hugh O'Neill after Kinsale* (Armagh, 1986).

Lario de Oñate, M.C., *La colonia mercantil británica e irlandesa en Cádiz a finales del siglo XVIII* (Cádiz, 2001).

Laurent, Catherine and David, Helen (eds), *Irlande et Bretagne: vingt siècles d'histoire* (Rennes, 1994).

Lennon, Colm, *Sixteenth-century Ireland: the incomplete conquest* (Dublin, 1994).

Lyons, Mary Ann, *Franco-Irish relations, 1500–1610: politics, migration and trade* (Woodbridge, 2003).

MacDonnell, Hector, *The Wild Geese of the Antrim MacDonnells* (Dublin, 1996).

McCavitt, John, *The Flight of the Earls* (Dublin, 2002).

O Connell, Patricia, *The Irish college at Alcalá de Hernares, 1649–1785* (Dublin, 1997).

O Connell, Patricia, *The Irish college at Lisbon, 1590–1834* (Dublin, 2001).

O Connell, Patricia, *The Irish college at Santiago de Compostela, 1605–1769* (Dublin, 2007).

O'Connor, Thomas (ed.), *The Irish in Europe, 1580–1815* (Dublin, 2001; repr. 2006).

O'Connor, Thomas, *Irish Jansenists, 1600–70. Religion and politics in Flanders, France, Ireland and Rome* (Dublin, 2008).

O'Connor, Thomas and Lyons, Mary Ann (eds), *Irish migrants in Europe after Kinsale, 1602–1820* (Dublin, 2003).

O'Connor, Thomas and Lyons, Mary Ann (eds), *Irish communities in early modern Europe* (Dublin, 2006).

Ó Dúshláine, Tadhg, *An Eoraip agus litríocht na Gaeilge, 1600–1650* (Dublin, 1987).

Ó Muraíle, Nollaig (ed.), *Turas na dTaoiseach nUltach as Éirinn. From Ráth Maoláin to Rome. Tadhg Ó Cianáin's contemporary narrative of the journey into exile of the Ulster chieftains and their followers, 1607–8 (The so-called 'Flight of the Earls')* (Rome, 2007).

O'Sullivan, Patrick (ed.), *The Irish world wide. I. Patterns of migration* (London, 1992).

Pařez, Jan and Kuchařová, Hedvika, *Hyberni v Praze – Éireannaigh i bPrág: Dějiny františkánské koleje Neposkvrněného početí Panny Marie v Praze, 1629–1786* (Prague, 2001).

Recio Morales, Óscar, *El Socorro de Irlanda en 1601 y la contribución del ejército a la integración social de los irlandeses en España* (Madrid, 2002).

Recio Morales, Óscar, *Irlanda en Alcalá: la comunidad irlandesa en la Universidad de Alcalá y su proyección europea, 1579–1785* (Alcalá, 2003).

Robinson-Hammerstein, Helga (ed.), *Migrating scholars: lines of contact between Ireland and Bohemia* (Dublin, 1998).

Schüller, Karin, *Die Beziehungen zwischen Spanien und Irland im 16. und 17. Jahrhundert: Diplomatie, Handel und die soziale Integration katholischer Exultanten* (Münster, 1999).

Stradling, Robert A., *The Spanish monarchy and Irish mercenaries. The Wild Geese in Spain, 1618–68* (Dublin, 1994).

Swords, Liam (ed.), *The Irish–French connection, 1578–1978* (Paris, 1978).

Villar García, María Begoña, *La emigración irlandesa en el siglo XVIII* (Málaga, 2000).

Villar García, María Begoña and Pezzi Cristóbal, P. (eds), *Los extranjeros en la España moderna* (2 vols, Málaga, 2003).

Walsh, T.J., *The Irish Continental college movement* (Cork, 1973).